Boss

Boss

The Story of S.F.B. Morse,
the Founder of Pebble Beach

Charles Osborne

Del Monte Publishing Co.
2018

Boss
Copyright © 2018 Charles Osborne
All rights reserved

Photo and illustration credits are on page 142.

Published in the United States by
Del Monte Publishing Co.
Pebble Beach, California

ISBN 978-0-692-06471-9

Cover and book design
by Lucky Valley Press
Jacksonville, Oregon
www.luckyvalleypress.com

Photograph of the author by Ethan A. Russell

Colorization of black and white cover photo
by Jim Dultz

Portrait of S.F.B. Morse on the back cover by Van Megert, used by permission.

Printed in the United States of America on acid-free paper that meets the Sustainable Forestry Initiative® Chain-of-Custody Standards. www.sfiprogram.org

Distributed internationally by Ingram

Dedication

I would like to dedicate "Boss" to my mother, first known as Mary Morse, then Mary Morse Osborne and Mary Morse Shaw. She was a great help with old stories about growing up in the "Splendid Isolation" of Pebble Beach…kissing Errol Flynn, decorated by Salvador Dali and hugged by Johnny Weissmuller ("he had such big arms"). She even knew what Boss's favorite bourbon was (*Old Grand-Dad* of course).

Acknowledgments

I want to thank members of my family for their help and support on this book. Firstly, and most significantly, my wife Karen for everything that she does for me, then my sister Ellen for her edits, her husband Jim Dultz who colorized the cover photo, my daughter Sarah for her support, my sons Matt, Jesse and Ian for their enthusiasm, and my cousins Sammy 3, Michael Hooker, Janie Roland and Rickie Morse for their stories.

Sandy Leader was the first editor and gave me critical guidance. Myra Goodman was my first reader and inspired me to go on. Ethan Russell helped enormously and Skip Lloyd asked the first question, "What motivated Sam Morse?"

My thanks to Ginna and David Gordon of Lucky Valley Press, book and cover designers and my guides through the printing process; to historians Neal Hotelling of the Pebble Beach Company, a great help, and John Sanders of the Hotel Del Monte.

And thank you to photo archivists Barbara Briggs-Anderson of Loon Hill.com, keeper of the Spike Graham collection, and to Pat Hathaway of California Views.

"Without Sam Morse, Pebble Beach
would be a West Coast Coney Island."
– Bing Crosby

"For 45 years one man stood
between 11 square miles of beauty
and any attempt to mar it."
– *Saturday Evening Post*, 1965

"He is an artist who has spent a lifetime
painting a 20,000 acre canvas."
– Jack Morse
*at a ceremony honoring his father
as the outstanding citizen of the
Monterey Peninsula in 1965*

Oil pastel painting of the Lone Cypress by S.F.B. Morse

Contents

Photographs and Illustrations

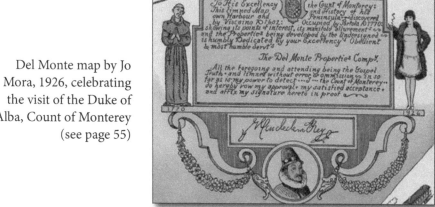

Del Monte map by Jo Mora, 1926, celebrating the visit of the Duke of Alba, Count of Monterey (see page 55)

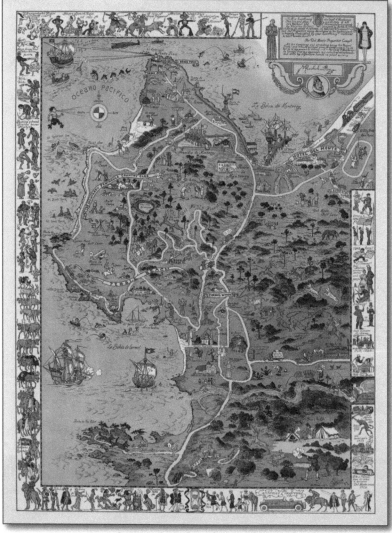

(View enlarged section on page 68)

The Beginning

Cheaters, Liars and Thieves

California in the late 19th and early 20th centuries was ripe for plundering. Vast wealth was being created, the population exploding, land being despoiled, and the rule of law questionable. At the turn of the century the state government was in the pocket of the railroad barons, crooked land grabbers and development schemers, and in San Francisco a bribe-taking racketeer ran the town.

Meanwhile a ruthless businessman bought up almost all of the Monterey Peninsula on the central California coast as payment of a legal bill.

By 1915, new communities along the central coast had a familiar layout—small lots and small houses crammed next to each other from the edge of the sea to the highway. Developers were after the quick buck, and this was how to do it. It was about to happen to Pebble Beach when Sam Morse entered the picture.

Proposal for a 400-lot development where the Pebble Beach Golf Links now are.

Preface

The Imagination of Sam Morse

"Sam Morse could out-imagine anyone," said Herb Cerwin, Del Monte PR man, drinking buddy and friend. Cerwin was right and he could have added that Morse turned these thoughts into reality.

Morse imagined a place with a pristine coastline, green-belted and free of buildings. He imagined creating a playground for his wealthy sporting pals and gals. He also imagined he could go the distance with Kid McCoy, a professional boxer who took on all comers.

His imagination never stopped sparking and he made things happen through force, charm, determination, teamwork and grit. It wasn't always smooth sailing, but it usually turned out to his liking, and he did go the distance (three rounds) in the ring with McCoy.

This is the story of my grandfather, S.F.B. Morse, founder of Pebble Beach, California, my personal hero and an icon of the good life in his time. He was a classic big fish in a small pond, but a beautiful pond and he made that pond even more desirable. He dominated the Monterey Peninsula for fifty years and surprisingly, he was extremely well thought of by most everyone. His vision of land conservation was the basis for the creation of one of the most attractive pieces of real estate in the world.

"How are you related to the man who invented the telegraph?" he was often asked. "All us Morses are related," he'd growl, and that was the end of that.

I am an investment advisor by profession and an historian by avocation. I was driven to this book because friends suggested I write down my grandfather's stories and I wanted to know who this man really was. His presence loomed large in my early life and continues to this day. It is strange to be in your grandfather's shadow as you approach your 70th birthday, but his was a very long shadow.

I grew up next to the 1st hole of the legendary Pebble Beach golf course. My grandfather lived on the other side of the fairway next door to my best friend, Lawson (Lawsy) Little III, son of a U.S. Open winner. My mother also grew up there, essentially as an only child, on the 18th fairway.

Someone once asked her what that was like. She called it "splendid isolation."

Monterey Peninsula

The Monterey Peninsula on the Central California coast is all that people say it is. The air is clean, moist, and pure. The temperature is moderate and the scenery spectacular. There is something about this coast that delights artists, photographers and everyone who visits or lives here. The shoreline is dramatic: jagged black and brown granite and limestone rocks stand against the relentless surf. The beaches have soft pure white sand and the bluffs above the ocean are framed in picturesque Monterey Cypress. The blue Pacific rolls in the background.

On top of these natural wonders the cultivated green of the golf courses in Pebble Beach accent the shoreline. Large homes are set back behind the golf courses so the coastline is undisturbed. Sports clubs and the equestrian center are nearby. The sounds of golf balls being thwacked, sails luffing, rackets plapping, horses snorting and children splashing show the joy of use intended for the place. Without Sam Morse and his vision we would not have this greatest meeting in the world of man, land and sea.

When Sam arrived on the Monterey Peninsula in 1915 to take over the Pacific Improvement Company, Pebble Beach was practically empty, with a few log houses, the original log Del Monte Lodge and the remains of a Chinese fishing village where the Beach Club is now. Much of the property was either sand dunes, dense forests or swamps. The shoreline was too rocky and too exposed for commercial purposes and it was famously foggy in the summer. In short there were far more opportunities for quick development elsewhere, but nowhere else held Sam's interest. It was a classic case of the right man in the right place at the right time.

Sam was more artist than investor, more conservationist than developer, but he was definitely all those things. He had a painterly vision for the Monterey Peninsula and deliberately set about to achieve it. I say he was an artist due to his temperament as well as his ability to execute. An investor is dispassionate and analytical while an artist is anything but that. Sam was passionate about the lands he acquired in 1919 and he let that passion rule his life. He wanted to create a Newport on the West Coast with large homes and a focus on sports and the outdoors. He made his living by developing property, and he did it slowly and carefully, always keeping his vision in mind. While Newport has declined, Pebble Beach has maintained its panache due to careful planning. All details were Sam's concern. He personally approved the design of every house built in Pebble Beach and every tree cut down from 1919 to 1969.

Physically he was imposing: tall, good-looking, barrel- chested and very strong, with deep set, clear blue eyes, a broken nose and a prominent chin. His daily uniform was a bow tie and tweed jacket. He liked to show off his strength and masculinity at parties by ripping phone books in half and telling football and cowboy stories. But he also told me once that if I went into business I should have art in my life for balance. He liked people and wanted people to like him. Others enjoyed his company, and he was extremely loyal to his friends.

As a grandfather, he was distant but friendly. He was fun to be with and had nicknames for each of us. Mine was Charles Disgustus (instead of my middle name Devens), Polly was Polly Wolly Doodle. My three sisters and I were the only ones of his ten grandchildren who were reared in Pebble Beach, but we saw him infrequently. When we did see him, it was special. He liked telling stories and giving advice. But he was not someone you dropped in on.

When I, as a senior in college, and was about to marry my first wife, he wrote a letter suggesting I get a job before I took this big step. He included a nice check anyway. As I was researching his life I found that he too had gotten married before he had a job and that, like mine, his marriage did not last, and he got a big check, too.

He was a man of his times who loved to paint and write, but didn't mind getting into a barroom brawl. I am told he sought them out. He loved the women in his life and enjoyed male company whether it was at the barbershop, the bar, the corral, the boxing ring or the boardroom. He was stern with his family as his parents were with him.

He believed education was the key to his success, not so much the schools he attended, Andover and Yale, but the people he met at those places. He was voted "most popular" during his senior year in college, but by his own admission he was not a great student.

He often referred to two early periods in his life when he told stories or was making a point. The first, when he played football at Yale and the second, when he ran a ranch in the California Central Valley. Football taught him teamwork and resiliency, ranching gave him perspective and insights into management and business. Both experiences taught him much and he applied this knowledge throughout his life. Water and access, he used to tell me, are the keys to development in California.

He generated a lot of publicity in his lifetime, from college days through the pinnacle of his career, and much was written about him, including several biographies (unpublished), newspaper and magazine stories and three versions of his "memoirs." I researched public records and interviews with friends and acquaintances, including his daughter Mary (my mother, now 96 and still living in Pebble Beach). His correspondence is at Stanford University in the Green Library special collections. Some of his letters to and from celebrities and politicians and his old diaries and photo albums, which provide a glimpse into his private life, are in my collection. He was a great storyteller and some of his stories are verbatim.

A newspaper dubbed him "The Duke of Del Monte" and although he pretended to be embarrassed by the title, I believe he liked it. Del Monte was more than a chunk of some of the most beautiful land on the planet. It was a style of life that included golf, tennis, polo, beautiful mansions and beautiful people having a good time. He enjoyed being in charge of that. In fact he wanted people to damn well know he was in charge. *Damn* was one of his favorite words.

He died when I was 22 years old while I was studying art at the University of California at Los Angeles, living above a merry-go-round on the Santa Monica Pier and working as a cue-card boy at NBC, none of which really met with my grandfather's approval. Still, the man was a big influence in my life and in the lives of many others, a benevolent despot who ruled the Monterey Peninsula.

Signature stamp from his book collection

His friends called him Sam and his employees called him Mr. Morse. People referred to him as S.F.B., and that is how he stylishly signed his paintings and documents.

The family called him Boss.

– Charles Osborne
2018

The sixth hole of the Pebble Beach Golf Links as it looks today. Compare this photo with the plan on page xiv showing the 1915 proposal for a development on this site.

Samuel Finley Brown Morse (1885-1969) in 1924, age 39

Chapter One

The Shaping of the Man - Newtonville, Massachusetts

Samuel Finley Brown Morse was born on July 18, 1885, the youngest son and sixth child of seven, to a Civil War veteran and an artist mother. This particular pairing of fighter and painter set the tone for Sam's whole life.

He grew up in Newtonville, Massachusetts, a sleepy suburb of Boston where his father commuted by train to his law office. Sam went to school at Andover and then, like many of his classmates, on to Yale. The family had a summer camp in Maine where he learned to ride, canoe and enjoy the outdoors, as well as listen to stories from old-timers.

Sam believed education and football were the keys to his early life. Education opened his world and introduced him to the right people. Football taught him leadership and how to get up after he was hit. Although his schools were typical enclaves for the wealthy and well connected, Sam did not fall in that category. Although Sam's father went to Andover, he was not wealthy and his family connection was with only one man, a preacher. This sole connection leading to Sam's education began with his grandfather Peter Morse.

Peter Morse (1801-1879) was a ship's mate from Chester, New Hampshire, where this branch of Morses lived for many generations. He was a contemporary of his famous second cousin S.F.B. Morse of painting and telegraph fame. Both descended from Anthony Morse (1607-1677).

Peter, described by contemporaries as a "man of great firmness and decision," publicly demonstrated this trait at age 24 as first mate on a ship rounding Cape Horn.

The story goes like this:

On one of Peter's early voyages the captain was drunk as they rounded Cape Hope, one of the most dangerous places on earth for sailing. In his stupor, the captain gave orders the first mate Morse knew would result in disaster. Morse told the crew not to obey the captain. Instead he confined the captain to quarters and took over. This bold act could be construed as mutiny, a hanging offense, if they were so fortunate as to survive the storms. They did survive, and upon their return to Boston, the captain wanted to charge Morse with this crime. Rev. Charles Finney (1792-1875), a young missionary who was on board and witnessed the encounter with the captain interceded, declaring that his "life had been saved by Morse." He made such a strong case that the ship's owner, Robert Gould Shaw, agreed to drop the charges and instead dismissed the captain, putting Morse in charge of the ship. A grateful Rev. Finney furthermore promised to educate any sons of Morse.

George Washington Morse 1845-1905

Capt. Peter Morse retired from the sea and became the postmaster in Lodi, Ohio. He married and had six children. His eldest son George was born in Lodi in 1845. In July of 1855, Peter sent young George, age 10, to Haverhill Academy, the Oberlin College prep school where Rev. Finney was president. George attended Haverhill for two years and then transferred to Phillips Academy, Andover.

George Washington Morse
(1845-1905) in 1861, age 15

In May of 1861, at age 15, George left school to join the Massachusetts 2nd Infantry to fight in the Civil War. Four years later at the end of this war in which millions of Americans died, he was one of 67 of the original 800 members in the regiment to survive intact and be honorably discharged.

The war was rough on young George. He experienced five major battles: Bull Run, Fredericksburg, Chancellorsville, Gettysburg, and Antietam. He was wounded twice and captured twice and incarcerated in the notorious Belle Isle and Libby prisons, foul and cruel places.

This was best described by a doctor of the time. Dr. Peter DeWitt at Jarvis Hospital examined soldiers released from Belle Isle and described them as being "in a semi-state of nudity... laboring under such diseases as chronic diarrhea, phthisis pulmonalis, scurvy, frost bites, general debility caused by starvation, neglect and exposure... They were filthy in the extreme, covered in vermin... nearly all extremely emaciated; so much so they had to be cared for even like infants."

Libby Prison was worse: a converted three-story warehouse holding 1,000 prisoners in eight small rooms open to the elements with never enough food or medical supplies. It was considered the second worse prison in the Confederate system, with Andersonville taking the prize.

George escaped from Belle Isle and exchanged out of Libby weighing only 95 pounds. After a short period of recovery, he was back in his regiment and soon sent back to New York to put down the draft riots. Sam said his father G.W. was a stern parent and one can see why.

During the war, George Morse rose in rank from drummer boy to brevet captain. In 1864 he marched "to the sea" through Georgia with Gen. William Tecumseh Sherman, an historic and reviled journey that left a trail of destruction. When he arrived in Atlanta, Sherman ordered all the industrial sites and the railroad yard destroyed, but to leave the business district and homes alone. His chief engineer heated rails red hot and wrapped them around trees; holes were punched in boilers; smokestacks pulled down, and all devices of machinery were disabled. They put the torch to passenger depots, roundhouses, machine shops and most of the hotels. Firebugs went to work on some of the buildings the general had not intended to burn. In all, 1,800 buildings including the business district were destroyed by fire.

Sherman (a former resident of Monterey, California) elevated the then Lt. George Morse to brevet captain and left him behind in Atlanta as an assistant to Provost Marshal Charles Fessenden Morse, a distant relative and fellow Bostonian. George won few friends in the performance of his duties, and his superior Lt. Col. Morse was much despised by the citizens. Still George was respected and did his best to restore peace and order in that ravaged city.

G. W. Morse, 1864, age 19

Years later, after the war, George Morse returned to Atlanta for a business meeting. After the meeting, as was the custom of the day, the men got together for dinner. The host introduced George as "someone who has been here before." The room was amused with the understatement as everyone there knew that G.W. had been with Sherman, but he stood up and addressed the group:

"Gentlemen, it is true that I was ordered to a do a job and I did it. It is also true that if I was born down here with you I would have been fighting along side you, because after all, we had nothing to do with the war except to fight it. If you, on the other hand had been born in Boston, we would have been fighting on the same side.

"But gentlemen, I want to add this thought. As I remember Atlanta when I first saw it, and now see the beautiful city you have built here, I am tempted to go back to Boston and recommend to my constituents that we send down here for a delegation to burn Boston to the ground and then have you rebuild it."

The group laughed in delight with the amusing twist and with the idea of doing it.

George returned to Andover after the war in 1865 and completed high school, most likely difficult for a young man experienced in the horrors of war, but he was a determined fellow. He went on to Dartmouth and Harvard and studied law in a local practice. He became a successful businessman and lawyer and married Sam's mother Clara Boit.

The Boits

Clara Boit was the granddaughter of another seaman of repute, Captain John Boit (1767-1827), skipper of the Union.

Captain Boit was involved in the first Indian war in the Pacific Northwest and was fifth mate on the Columbia Rediviva skippered by Captain John Gray in what is now Vancouver, British Columbia, in 1792. They were trading primarily for beaver and otter pelts as well as other hides and Captain Gray thought he had been cheated by the local Indians and decided to teach them a lesson. He had his sailors shoot their cannon at the deserted Indian village and destroy it. Peace with the local tribes was shattered and it became dangerous to continue trading. Boit felt that Gray had significantly overreacted and he was very public about it. He kept accurate logs of his journeys, this one becoming a public document. Despite his indignation, nothing was done. Gray was just one of many sea captains who took pelts and treated the natives badly.

Sam's ancestor Captain Boit safely returned to Boston. The owner of the ship (his brother-in law) was impressed by Boit's log and his good work as a fifth mate. He made the 20-year-old Boit captain of the 90-ton sloop Columbia. Captain Boit then retraced his prior voyage and was the first to circumnavigate the globe in a sloop-rigged ship. His "Log of the Union" was published and became a bestseller. Boit later retired to Newton, married, and had several children. His wife, Amanda Berry, was from nearby Bridgetown, Massachusetts. Their youngest son, James, was the father of Clara.

Clara Boit Morse (1851-1919)

Clara was an accomplished artist as well as mother of seven children, five girls and two boys. She lived a long and full life, outliving her husband by 14 years. She had her hands full with a strong-willed husband and seven active children plus her painted ceramics and other media. She may have colorized the photo of herself included here.

She died in 1919 in Los Angeles while visiting her daughters, Rosa and Genevieve, known as Johnnie.

Four of George and Clara's seven children moved to California. Johnnie moved first to Los Angeles then to Monterey after her husband, Thomas Christian, died. Rosa and Harry lived in Southern California, Rosa in Los Angeles, and Harry owned a ranch near Tehachapi. Sam moved to Merced in 1907. In photographs Harry has the look of a resentful older brother and a bully, possibly the reason Sam had little contact with him despite both living in California.

Sam liked to say he grew up in the horse and buggy era and he would point out all the changes since he was a boy in the 1890s: no cars or airplanes, and radios and television were just fantasy. His namesake and distant relative invented the telegraph 50 years before he was born. Thomas Edison was well-known by this time, and his wizardry was still unfolding while the lesser known Nicola Tesla was considered insane.

Sam Morse embraced the new but preferred some of the old. Airplane rides deprived him of looking at the scenery. Cars were convenient but noisy, and he always loved to sit in the saddle of a spirited horse.

The one surviving recording of his voice was made late in his life and only discovered recently. During a remodel of the home of the Monterey Peninsula Herald reporter and editor Jimmy Costello, contractors tore down a wall. Hidden inside the wall was an old-fashioned tape recorder with a tape inside containing a conversation between Sam and Costello. Sam was reading from his memoirs but at some point the machine stopped and he asked Jimmy, "Are you sure that damn thing is working? I'd hate to be making a blank tape." He referred to most new technology like tape recorders as "that damn thing." He was over 80 at the time and not alone at railing against the new.

Sam's father George was a stern parent. Those four years between the ages of 15 and 19, when he fought alongside grown men and survived many hardships, clearly made a lasting impression on him. Both Sam and his brother Harry Morse grew up tough and disciplined. I have no doubt the two boys relished a good fight, with Sam rarely coming out on top. Still he had no complaints about his childhood. His father was a successful lawyer in his firm and was an active in business. George was part of the group that installed the trolley system in Newtonville and later the town's electrification.

George Morse died in 1905 while in Marseille sailing along the French Riviera, having taken a leave from his law firm, Morse, Loomis and Lane. Sam was a sophomore at Yale and soon realized he was on his own.

G.W. Morse in Marseille, 1905

Chapter Two

Andover and New Haven - Football

S am always wanted to play football, which concerned his mother because he was not a big kid. She clearly wanted to protect her youngest son and knew about the violence and injuries incurred playing the game. She tried to steer Sam away from it but her warnings that he was too slight had the opposite effect: he started training and building himself up with exercise, something he continued to do for the rest of his life. In 1903 he made the Andover team as a running back. He also learned to box. He enjoyed rough sports and physical punishment, trying mostly to dish it out but when the tables turned he also admired the victor.

Sam at Andover, age 17

The sons of many Civil War vets embraced football as a way to prove their mettle, as no war was available. The rugged game was played as if a battle were being waged. Eleven men lined up against another eleven and they pounded into each other. There was no passing, no helmets, and no real strategy. The rules were constantly evolving.

Seventeen young men died in 1905 playing football, and there was a movement to ban it from college sports. Teddy Roosevelt loved the game and embraced the forward pass as a way to reduce injuries. Teddy was extremely popular when Sam was growing up and clearly was an idol to Sam and other young men. Sam was thrilled when he met him years later at the outbreak of World War I. Teddy even recruited Sam to be in his new Rough Riders, but the War Department nixed the idea of the now elderly Roosevelt recreating the charge at San Juan Hill.

Walter Camp, father of American football and a former coach at Yale, devised several new rules to make the game safer. Also, Pop Warner at the Carlyle Indian School was a great innovator of the game at many levels. He perfected the forward pass with the adaptation of putting a spiral on the ball. Initially a dropped pass incurred a penalty, a rule quickly overturned. The ball was rounder than it is now and difficult to throw, so the concept of the forward pass started slowly.

Warner's development of the spiral was his crowning achievement. This allowed his smaller and less experienced Native American kids to take on the bigger and tougher boys at established schools such as Yale and the University of Chicago.

Sam told me a story about when the boys from Cambridge University came to Yale to play American football and then to take on the Americans in Rugby. Although the Englishmen did well in football, they had no defense for the forward pass. The Americans lost the rugby game, but held the day in football. This was important to him for some reason. I imagine because we all still viewed the English as superior sportsmen.

Even after Sam could no longer play, he took an interest in the sport. While in the California Central Valley working for W. H. Crocker he took over the coaching of the Visalia football team. The boys were not the greatest athletes, but one of them had a good leg and could kick the ball long. Sam incorporated this into the strategy and the team would often kick on second and third downs, surprising their opponents. They went on to the league championship and even beat much larger schools like Lick-Wilmerding of San Francisco.

Yale

S am went straight from Andover to Yale as did several of his classmates. He was popular at both schools due to his determination, good looks and football, but not for his scholarship. Studying was not his focus. He truly believed his friends were more important than any knowledge he might acquire. He made friends easily and was loyal to them. He joined the semi-secretive Skull and Bones Society and was also known to carouse around town looking for girls or a fight, preferably with a Harvard man.

Sam was voted most popular in his class and as captain of the best football team in the country, he was known nationally. There were no professional football teams at the time and yet the country was fascinated by the sport. Yale was among the top teams and in 1907, undefeated. Sam was somewhat controversial as he played the game with rough violence, as if he were re-fighting the Civil War. At the 1907 Harvard-Yale game ("The Game") he was disqualified for a hit on an opponent.

In those days, many of the players were on both offense and defense. Sam was a running back but also played linebacker. The Harvard halfback, John Wendell, was lined up opposite Sam, who put a vicious hit on him. The ref thought it was too much and kicked Sam out of the game. The next day Wendell wrote Sam a letter with a copy to the Boston Register saying the hit was legal and that Sam put his arm out to ward him off and had not struck him as the ref ruled. He told Sam that he bore no ill will and looked forward to a continued rivalry.

Sam told a Yale story while I received a hair cut in a barbershop. There were several men waiting for Mike the barber to finish

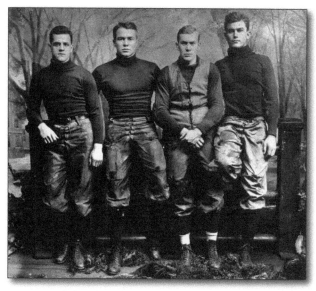

Yale backs 1906, Sam is second from left

giving me "short back and sides." There were two stools and four chairs for waiting and Sam and two men were in the chairs. Something came up about Sam's days playing football and whether or not he had played against black athletes. This was in the late 1950s and Rosa Parks had sat in the front of that bus in 1955 and Sam's former friend, Earl Warren, had presided over "Brown vs. Board of Education." Sam responded to the question of playing against African-Americans with this anecdote:

Boston Post, Sunday November 25, 1906 "The Game"

"When I was captain of the Yale team, we played a school that had "colored" men on the team. As the game went on, it was clear that some of the Southern boys on the Yale team were being overly aggressive towards the black players: piling on after the play and vicious out of control hits. I told the boys to calm down or the ref may make them forfeit or remove the violators from the game.

"Just before half time, I went over to the ref and said, 'Ref, I have to apologize for some of my boys. They're from the south and are having trouble playing against coloreds.' The ref paused a minute and then, in a thick Southern drawl said, 'Y'all don't worry about a thing. Just keep on playing football.'"

After the death of his father in his sophomore year, Sam started looking to his friends more than his family. Many of the young men he met at Yale stayed friends for life, including Bill and Templeton Crocker as well as Harris Hammond. Yale, being an elite institution, was fodder for

Yale Cartoon by a classmate, 1906

Sam's ambition. He did not yet know what he wanted to do with his life, but he knew it was not in Boston. Many of his friends such as Hammond and Crocker came from California and the idea of wide open spaces and escaping the stuffy confines of New England was very appealing. But first he felt he needed a wife.

Anne Thompson

Right after his senior year at Yale Sam married Anne Camden Thompson, an orphan born in Virginia and raised by her uncle in New Jersey. She was a strict Christian Scientist. They met through mutual friends, the particulars of which are lost. She was petite and pretty and physically, Sam towered over her but they were an attractive couple. Initially he was devoted to her, but later realized he had married too young. Perhaps he was inspired by the $500 prize for the first member of the class of 1907 to get married, which he won. Sam hated to lose at anything.

They were married in a private home in New Jersey and after a brief honeymoon, the couple went west to Sam's first job.

As Sam approached graduation he began to think of his career. Boston was not attractive to him and there were no jobs waiting for him there. His lawyer father had died and there may have been work at his old firm, but he described himself as a mediocre student and had no intention of studying law. He was impatient to get on with life. He admired the parents of several of his friends, especially those from California. (John Hays Hammond, the father of one of his friends, Harris Hammond, was teaching at Yale at the time. He had grown up in California and prior to his teaching position had a fascinating career in mining). The great fire and earthquake that leveled San Francisco had perked up his interest in the West, that and books by Mark Twain and Bret Harte. All these elements steered him to the Wild West for his future.

Sam in 1906, voted most
popular in his class

Sam and Anne's wedding, 1907
Clara Morse is on his left

Chapter Three

The Wild West; Hammond; Delano

Hammond, Sam's first employer, was a colorful fellow who was once sentenced to death in South Africa and at another time fought off revolutionaries in Mexico. A famed mining engineer, he made a fortune before he was 40 and was associated with several ruthless entrepreneurs.

Hammond originally came from California, the child of hopeful Forty-Niners who immigrated from Texas. At a young age and after mining school, John worked for George Hearst, father of William Randolph Hearst. Hearst and his partner, Lloyd Tevis, founded both Anaconda Copper and Homestake Mining, still two of the largest mining companies in the world. Tevis, a man who could think "five times faster than anyone else in San Francisco" was the financier. Hearst was the miner, and a very good one as history has shown.

John Hayes Hammond (1855-1936)
Time Magazine, May 10, 1926
"Most radically democratic millionaire"

Hearst sent Hammond to Sonora, Mexico, in 1882, just as a revolution was breaking out. Porfirio Diaz was consolidating his control over Mexico and had become quite unpopular in parts of the country. Only a few years earlier, Diaz rose to power after the overthrow of the much-despised French-appointed Emperor Maximilian on Cinco de Mayo. But his subsequent rebellion against his former ally Benito Juarez did not sit well in Sonora. After Diaz took over the government in 1877, he ruled with an iron hand. Diaz served seven terms as El Presidente, despite Juarista revolutionaries.

Business was good for Diaz and his friends, like Hearst, but not so much for the campesinos, the native farm laborers. Hearst profited nicely during the dictator's regime and later so did Hammond. When Hammond and his young family were holding off the Juaristas in their little adobe, Diaz came to his rescue. Hammond never forgot the favor. Years later in 1909, Hammond helped save the life of Diaz and President William Taft at an unprecedented meeting of the two leaders in El Paso, Texas. Hammond hired the famous ranger Frederick Russell Burnham to safeguard the two presidents. The rangers foiled an assassination attempt by spotting and apprehending an armed man lying in wait.

Hammond returned to California in 1883 and worked as a consulting engineer for the Big Four's Central Pacific Railroad. He left to go to South Africa in 1893 to develop gold mines there for Cecil Rhodes's British South Africa Company and became Rhodes's chief mining engineer in charge of all his gold and diamond mines.

Rhodes was at odds with the Boer government and did his best to get rid of the government led by Paul Kruger. He had his man in the Transvaal organize a revolt which failed. This was not a good move. An unsympathetic Boer-dominated court sentenced Hammond and other conspirators to death. After Hammond paid a large fine and spent three months in a filthy jail, President Kruger commuted the sentence. Hammond left South Africa for England and never returned. He was wealthy and famous at this point and acted as a consultant as well as an investor in mines in the U.S., Africa and Mexico.

In 1902, Hammond became a professor of mining engineering at Yale University, where Sam met him through his son, Harris. Hammond, Sr., was not your typical professorial type. He continued to be actively involved in managing his fortune, investing in real estate and consulting in mining properties for the Guggenheim family. His contract with the Guggenheims was very lucrative, guaranteeing an income of $100,000 a year plus a share of the profits. He also became interested in politics and made a failed run at the vice-presidency in 1908.

Hammond was impressed with the rough and ambitious young Sam and offered him a job in either the Sudan or in California. Sam and Anne talked it over and decided California sounded better than the burning sands of Africa, so they chose the job they thought would be on the west coast. Clearly their grasp of geography needed help as Hammond sent them to the town of Visalia in California's extremely hot San Joaquin Valley. They had no idea.

In September of 1907 the young couple traveled west by train for a week from Chicago and then over the Rockies and the Sierra Nevada to get to California and they saw much of the beauty of the land. The West was wild and largely unpopulated, the mountains majestic, the valleys endless and the clichés unbounded. The west was big, beautiful and ripe.

Sam was ready to taste this fruit. Hammond had been developing property in Merced and Kern counties as well as building up a water and power company. He had two rules he drilled into Sam: You must have an adequate water source and be sure your access to the land is legal. Water and Access.

Hammond had started the Mt. Whitney Power Company as his base investment. Further to the south he was developing a 4,000-acre tract near Delano that he wanted Sam to oversee. Although water was not a problem, and Hammond was assured of access to the land, he did have one major problem: rabbits.

Rabbits

Delano is a hot dusty place on flats below the Sierra Nevada. With no natural predators the rabbit population exploded. There were so many rabbits on the property they undermined the infrastructure, causing potholes in roads, pipes to collapse and electrical poles to topple over. They made farming impossible. Sam's every attempt to get rid of the rabbits failed. He hired a hundred cowboys, lined them up five miles across and had them stampede the rabbits into a chute which in turn fed into a large cage. He called it a "memorable sight:" the cowboys stamping around and the rabbits fleeing like "waves in the ocean" across the plains of Delano.

Ultimately they came back and Sam gave up, realizing that the project was ill-timed. It was a defeat for Sam but he learned a great deal about development, engineering, water management and rabbits.

During his time with Hammond he took a trip to Sonora, Mexico, to tour Hammond's ranching and mining interests there. He had an interesting trip during a period when the government seemed to change daily and bandits ruled the north near the border. The bandits called themselves revolutionaries, but terrorists is a better description. One, Pancho Villa, actually succeeded for a short time and headed the government. It was a wild time.

One night, there was a fiesta in the town and Sam, a curious fellow, went to see the action; not a safe thing to do in those times. The Yacqui Indians were a rough bunch with no love for Norte Americanos. Mexico and the U.S. were at war not that long ago and the revolutionary fervor with Pancho Villa and others made it unsafe for a gringo alone. Sam paid this no mind. He was a big strong guy with a lot of self-confidence, but he may have been misguided when he decided to go into a cantina.

He was enjoying the music and dancing at the fiesta when he noticed a man staring at him hard and muttering to his friends. Clearly the gentleman had been drinking and, although Sam did not speak any Spanish, he could sense an obvious threat. The man got up and pulled out a knife. He started right for Sam, waving the knife and sounding angry. Sam waited until the man got close and deftly grabbed the smaller man's wrist and held the knife up. He lifted the attacker's arm, pointed to the knife, and said to the man, "Cuanto?" The man, recognizing that Sam was offering him a chance to save face, replied, "Dos pesos."

The deal was done. Sam paid him the two pesos and took the knife. He said the blade was razor sharp. He considered it one of the best deals he ever made.

In 1910, Sam left Hammonds' Mount Whitney Power Company. He had contracted amoebic dysentery in Mexico and also had to have his appendix removed. He was quite ill. He went to San Francisco for the operations. He enjoyed working for Hammond but it was time to move on. The rabbits were the last straw. He learned a great deal about property development and water management under Hammond's guidance and Sam being ambitious was looking for more action. The bad news was that he was not sure what his next business would be: he was broke from the medical expenses and still recovering from his illnesses. Sam had a perforated intestine and a liver abscess resulting in three separate operations within a period of 17 days, including an appendectomy complicated by peritonitis.

San Francisco was the principal city in California in the late 1800s and into the 20th century. The city, as locals call it, had the money and the population to rule the state, but the state was in transition. There were a lot of contentious land claims still, as California was a work in progress. Mexican land claims were often ignored or decided by courts, biased in favor of the Yankees. Although it had been a state for 60 years, they were very rough years, with fierce battles over water, boundaries, access and other land use issues. For most of that time the railroad men, ruthless land barons and swindlers, made the laws.

Broke with no job and a 2-year-old child, Sam Jr., Sam spent what money he had on doctors and cures for his problems. He needed a plan and was organizing a loan company. Then he renewed his college friendship with his two Crocker friends, Templeton and W.W. (Bill), grandsons of the famous Charles Crocker, one of the Big Four and the primary builder of the Central Pacific Railroad.

Chapter Four

W.H. Crocker and Big Sam, the Cowboy;
Visalia and Merced

W.H. Crocker (Will) was the youngest son of Charles Crocker and carried on the old man's business interests for the family. He was head of the Crocker Bank, which grew to be one of the largest in California, eventually being absorbed by its crosstown rival Wells Fargo. Will was the father of Sam's Yale friend, Bill and guardian to his nephew and nieces, Sam's fellow Yalie, Templeton Crocker and his sisters, Jennie and Mary. Their parents had both died young and left them very rich orphans.

Among many other holdings, the Crockers owned a 65,000-acre ranch in the Central Valley near Merced called the Crocker-Huffman Ranch. The ranch operation was vast, including cattle, chickens and other livestock, plus a water company and a development company, but the operation as a whole was losing money. Crocker was upset over the latest report on the ranch and could not figure out how this operation he invested so much in could lose money.

Sam secured an invitation from Templeton to see Crocker to get him to invest in his mortgage company. After a brief interview it was clear Crocker had other plans. Knowing that Sam had worked in the Central Valley for Hammond, he sent him to Merced to report on what he found at the Crocker-Huffman Ranch.

Sam came back with a thorough review and several suggestions to improve operations, among them to get rid of the chicken business and to delay any further development. Crocker must have been impressed with the spirit and energy of this young man for he impulsively offered Sam the job of running the ranch operations. Sam was broke and nervous about his future and this looked like a godsend. He accepted the offer immediately. He made $250 a month from Hammond and Crocker offered him twice that. In addition he had housing, a car, a full staff, servants and plenty of cowboys. Most importantly, it was his operation to run. Sam was thrilled.

Sam loved the next five years as a cowboy businessman. He met real cowpokes and heard stories of the Old West, the not-too-distant past. He ran a vast cattle herd, had his pick of fine horses and spent a great deal of his time outdoors. He made deals, bought livestock and set up the land development and the water company, which eventually became the Merced Irrigation District.

Anne did not care much for the life there. She had a rambunctious second child in 1912, John Boit, known as Jack, and Sam was not often home. She was tired of the Central Valley and disappointed they had returned to it. The Central Valley was hotter and less pleasant than their images of palm trees dancing along the California coastline.

At every opportunity Anne had Sam drive the family to Monterey to stay at the Hotel Del Monte. When they crested the Pacheco Pass the family would cheer as they caught sight of the fog. But the ranch was Sam's job as well as their home, and he wanted to make it work.

Sam mastered the ranching business in the only way he could: he learned every part of it. He roped, he tied, he branded. He loved the rough physical nature of the ranch and every aspect of it.

S.F.B. Morse (left) inspecting cattle on the range at Dry Creek with his Cattle Superintendent Ken Safford - *Merced Historical Society, Courthouse Museum Collection*

One of Sam's experiences on the Ranch was a western version of fox hunting: coyote chasing, a favorite pastime. These thieving critters caused serious damage to livestock and running them down on horseback was considered great fun. The ranch had a pack of part Greyhound part Scottish Deerhound dogs. Four or five cowboys lined up, one to handle the dogs and the rest to chase down the coyotes. They ran full speed over rough terrain until either the dogs caught up with the coyotes or the coyotes got away. The chase usually lasted a mile or so.

On one occasion Sam chased a large male coyote by himself. The chase went on and covered several miles. Sam was exhausted and so was his horse. With the coyote just a few yards in front of them, Sam pulled up. The coyote, who was just as exhausted as they were, also stopped and rested. Sam looked over and saw the dead tired but brave animal. He pulled out his gun but could not go through with it. The critter had put up a good fight and deserved to live.

Sam never hunted again. One of his best pets was half-dog half-coyote. Faithful and easy to train, he looked like a small collie, but ran with his nose to the ground like a coyote. Sadly, one of Sam's own cowboys shot him, mistaking it for a wild coyote.

Sam went on long rides sometimes for weeks and listened to the stories of the old cowboys about famous cattle drives and the true wildness of the West.

One senior fellow was with the group that drove cattle up to Little Big Horn to make peace with the Sioux Indians after the battle with Custer. He told Sam that after they turned the herd over, the Indians slaughtered every animal on the spot. He had no idea why.

Another favorite story was the "Plate of Onions." Sam liked to tell this story as an example of the rough cowboy life of the past. The story goes as follows:

Two cowboys rode all day to another ranch in the same county to visit a girl who had attracted the interest of the younger cowboy. The girl's father was the owner of the ranch, but the family ate with the hands. The dinner was a little formal that night and awkward since the nervous young suitor could hardly speak. He did, however, ask for a second helping of onions. The older cowboy then said, "I can't think much of a man who would ride all day to see a girl and ask for a second helping of onions." There was laughter from all but not from the embarrassed young cowboy. He got up, strapped on his gun, and said, "Meet me outside!" to the older man.

The old cowboy waited a few minutes. He didn't believe he was really going to have a gunfight over his comment but the young man did not come back in so, shaking his head, he walked over to the coat rack and put on his belt and holster. He looked outside but could not see the other man. He went out the door, still not seeing his friend. The young cowboy was hiding behind a shed. He stepped out and shot him. The old cowboy did not die right away and shot and killed the young man. As the old cowboy lay dying he said, "I can't believe this was over a plate of onions."

Sam was fascinated with early Californio bandits, especially Joaquin Murrieta and Tiburcio Vasquez. In his mind these men were fighting for their land stolen by the early American settlers.

Sam was a romantic. After annexation and statehood all of the Spanish-era deeds were reviewed. Of course, there was a lot of chicanery and Californios were considered a lower class, especially if they were of Spanish descent. The bulk were of mixed blood and had been running Alta California after Mexico essentially abandoned governing it. They called themselves Californios. Many natives were cheated out of their land as the Americans controlled the police, the courts and the press. Sam thought they especially mistreated Vasquez. Later, Sam hired the great-nephew of Vasquez as a ranch hand and wrote a short fictional story about Tiburcio Vasquez.

In the story of Tiburcio Vasquez, Sam wrote the narrative in the first-person about a fictional rancher in Carmel Valley who befriended him. He romanticized the stagecoach robber while recognizing that Vasquez turned to crime rather than the courts to reclaim his lost land. Sam recounted the story told by Henry Miller, the Cattle King, of being robbed by Vasquez but then "borrowing $20" to get home. Years later, Miller saw Vasquez at a cantina and gave him $20, repaying his debt.

In the end of this fictional account, as in real life, Vasquez was caught and hung in San Jose.

Tiburcio Vasquez, bandit
(1835-1875)

Chapter Five

Ranching - The Boxer and the Bandit

S am learned the sweet science of boxing at Yale and enjoyed it. While at the ranch in Merced, Sam often boxed with some of the cowboys. They set up a ring in one of the barns, had the cook be the referee and did three-round bouts. In those times, fighting was considered part of growing up, as was "spare the rod, spoil the child." Boxing was another way to prove your manhood. He also didn't mind a good barroom brawl.

A former professional boxer named "Kid" McCoy heard about the boxing matches. At the time, he made a living traveling around California taking on all comers and betting they could not go the distance with him (three rounds). McCoy was an unsavory fellow: a few years later he murdered his fifth wife and got away with it. He too was a barroom brawler and liked to pick fights by lisping and pretending he was gay. Not tall but solidly built, he would insinuate himself into a conversation in a bar and insult people. Eventually a fight got started and McCoy would then beat up his victim. In sum, a nasty fellow.

One fight was memorable, the genesis of the phrase "the Real McCoy." It seems McCoy was about to get into it with a local man when the man's friend warned him against it. He told his buddy not to fight him because that was Kid McCoy. His friend ignored the advice saying, "That's not Kid McCoy! I've seen McCoy fight, and he's much bigger." Within minutes, McCoy connected with the man's chin, and as he was going down he was heard to say, "I guess that *is* the Real McCoy."

Sam got his chance with McCoy in 1915 at the opening of the Panama Pacific International Exposition in San Francisco. McCoy set up a tent giving boxing demonstrations at the fair. He was looking for a sparring

Kid McCoy (née Norman Selby, 1872-1940) on trial for murder

partner. Sam's friends goaded him into stepping up, which probably didn't take much encouragement.

Sam's experience as a boxer made him the logical one to fight McCoy. He was thirteen years younger and strong and quick, but McCoy was crafty, experienced and did not like to lose. Sam was clearly the loser in the sparring match against the wily veteran, but he went the three round distance. He landed a few punches and did not take too many himself. He and his friends went out later and celebrated. According to Sam he "managed to go the distance without too much damage."

MacFarlane

At about the same time there was a cattle rustler named Bob McFarlane or Mac, as he was known. Half Scottish and half Native American, he was a classic looking bad man with a dark scowling face and piercing blue eyes.

At the beginning of the last century cattle rustling was still a big problem in the West. Using a running iron, rustlers amended the brand to be unrecognizable by the owner. McFarlane, a particularly well known thief in the little town of Merced, was yet to be caught red-handed. Earlier in his life he killed four men, served time at San Quentin and bragged about it. He threatened and intimidated whoever bothered him.

Sam was fed up with losing cattle to rustlers and increased patrols and security. He had any butcher in the area who bought a side a beef first see the brand before completing the purchase. He offered rewards for information and was closing in on McFarlane when he got a call from a friend in a nearby town that Mac was telling everyone who would listen he was going to shoot that son-of-a-bitch Morse as soon as he could find him. McFarlane used the flimsy excuse that Morse cheated him out of his home.

He wanted to buy the shack he lived in on the part of the ranch being developed. He paid one of Sam's men $15 for it, but another agent sold the same property to someone else. Mac blamed Morse.

When Sam found out Mac was looking for him and threatening to kill him he immediately went to Mac's hovel to find him. When he arrived McFarlane was not there but Sam noticed the shack had only one entrance and no windows. If he could find Mac at home, he would have him trapped.

He had started to leave when he saw a buckboard with Mac driving heading his way. Sam could see he was armed to the teeth with a six shooter on his hip and a rifle in the wagon. Sam was not carrying a gun.

As Mac approached, he stopped next to Sam but did not get down from the wagon. Sam immediately spoke up, "I heard you were looking for me. If it is about that house, my men made a mistake, and I would like to return your $15." He held up the money and after a pause, Mac took it.

This of course was not what Mac was expecting. He thanked Sam and told him, "Mr. Morse, I would like to work for you. If you hired me I would guarantee no more cattle rustling on the ranch." Sam smiled and thanked Mac for his offer and said he would consider it.

Fortunately for Sam, he did not have to decline the offer. Unfortunately for McFarlane, he was shot and killed a few years later in a bar fight. Few were unhappy he was gone.

Sam enjoyed his time at the ranch and learned about management and men. He had been at the ranch for five years and operations were going smoothly. He dumped the chicken business, developed a profitable water company and was running 8,000 head of cattle and sometimes an even larger herd. Anne had her third child, a baby girl named Nancy, and she was done with the Central Valley. It was time for a vacation to San Francisco. They all wanted to go see the just-opened World's Fair.

Chapter Six

San Francisco 1915

The Panama-Pacific International Exhibition, San Francisco, 1915

Sam's boss, Will Crocker, was the chairman of the Panama-Pacific International Exhibition in San Francisco, a World's Fair theoretically celebrating the opening of the Panama Canal, but in reality, promoting the city. The earthquake and fire had been world news with "City destroyed" a typical headline and many felt San Francisco would never recover. The gold was pretty much gone and the devastation so vast the rebuild was uncertain.

The city fathers had other ideas. Will and other civic leaders wanted the world to know the city was rebuilding and still vital despite the earthquake and fire that leveled it in 1906. This was to be the big debut of the new city the world had written off.

After the earthquake the major bankers of the city were flooded with loan requests. They were Will Crocker (Crocker Bank), Amadeo Giannini (Bank of Italy), Richard Tobin (Hibernia Bank), Isaias Hellman (Wells Fargo) and Herbert Fleischhacker (Anglo California Bank). These men, more than city planners and civic leaders, were responsible for the rebuilding of San Francisco.

The earthquake and fire destroyed more than 25,000 buildings, city hall was corrupt and insurance companies were quibbling over details. Abraham "Boss" Ruef was running the show and controlling all new construction. If you wanted a permit you had to pay Ruef a "consulting fee." The whole city was subject to Ruef's greed.

Sam's soon-to-be new father-in-law, was indicted but later cleared of bribing Ruef in the "Parkside Scandal." W.H. Crocker was developing 400 acres near Golden Gate Park in 1907 and wanted United Railways to bring trolley service to the development. Most all the citizens wanted the trolleys to have underground power, but that was expensive. Boss Ruef ran the unions in San Francisco and thus controlled the reconstruction after the earthquake. The man who ran the trolley company, John Calhoun, hired Ford as his attorney. Ford delivered $200,000 in small bills to Ruef as a "legal fee," and the trolley cars were allowed to have the ugly overhead wires the citizens had objected to. During the eventual trial, Ruef admitted bribing the council but stated firmly that the money Ford delivered was entirely for legal fees. Ford was exonerated, but Ruef went to prison. He was the only one.

"ATONEMENT"
A cartoon from the San Francisco *Examiner*, May 16, 1907.

The World's Fair

The World's Fair, with its elaborate Maybeck buildings and Golden Gate waterfront vistas, proved to be a fabulous success. It showed the world that San Francisco had recovered from the earthquake and rebuilt herself.

The fair covered 636 acres of waterfront land now known as the Marina District. It lasted from February 20 to October 4, 1915. 24 countries were represented, significant given that WWI had started in 1914. The Liberty Bell was shipped out from Pennsylvania for display (the last time it ever left Philadelphia) and Southern Pacific loaned a locomotive, the "C.P. Huntington," as an exhibit, one of the first three engines of the Central Pacific Railroad.

The centerpiece of the fair was the Tower of Jewels, a construction rising 435 feet above ground encrusted with 100,000 cut diadems. When illuminated at night, the tower was spectacular. Bernard Maybeck designed the Palace of Fine Arts building, a permanent copy of which still stands today in the same place.

Over 18 million people traveled to see it and many of them took the train down the coast and stayed at the luxurious Hotel Del Monte, the dream child of Charles Crocker of the Big Four. Will Crocker wanted Sam to see the fair, but he also wanted to talk to him about the Pacific Improvement Company.

Chapter Seven

The Big Four and the Pacific Improvement Company

These four men, Leland Stanford, Collis Huntington, Charles Crocker and Mark Hopkins, amassed great wealth during the early days of Anglo California. Originally from upstate New York, they came to California for the gold but they found that selling shovels to the miners in Sacramento was more profitable. When the U.S. government was looking for a group to build the western portion of the transcontinental railroad, the "Associates," what they called themselves, formed the Central Pacific Railroad and got the contract. This proved lucrative and that is a major understatement. In 1880, it was estimated that each man was worth $40,000,000. To give the reader an idea of the scale of their wealth, just 20 years earlier the United States bought Alaska for $6,000,000.

Charles Crocker
(1822-1888)

Besides the $16,000 per mile reimbursement by the government for flat land railbuilding, they were granted an option to purchase a checkerboard of square-mile plots of land on each side of the line. Construction in the foothills was reimbursed at $32,000/mile and in the mountains at $64,000. The Associates formed a company to hold all these properties and companies that were non-rail assets. They called it the Pacific Improvement Company or the PIC. In California alone the PIC owned huge chunks of Monterey, Alameda, Santa Barbara, and San Mateo counties as well as Castle Crags and other properties.

Some of the wealth came from chicanery such as overstating the amount of double-paid difficult terrain they crossed. Per their surveys, the Sierra Nevada was twice its actual size and thus they received four times the regular agreed upon price per mile. Still this was nothing compared to what the Union Pacific did coming west.

Their scams included bribing senators and making the road wind when it could go straight thereby increasing the miles of track and thus their profit.

A second bit of now totally illegal profit enhancing was the import of Chinese coolie labor by Crocker. These men were essentially indentured servants working for practically nothing. Crocker, whose idea it was, estimated at a Congressional hearing that there were probably "10 to 20 thousand" coolies now in California. It is not quite so villainous as it sounds to modern ears, but there is no doubt that the treatment of the Chinese in California in the late 1800s was despicable.

The first construction employees of the railroad were mostly Irish men and Civil War vets who would drink and fight and run off to the gold fields as soon as they had a stake. Crocker had the idea of hiring Chinese, some were in California already. They were harshly discriminated against and could not hold jobs where white men worked. Persecution was rampant: white gangs would go into Chinatown and cut off pigtails. One man wrote in his diary that he "had a good day…shot a Chinaman." He was subsequently appointed the U.S. ambassador to Japan.

Crocker was eventually able to offer the Chinese workers a decent job with appropriate wages and he was powerful enough to bring it off. The working conditions were rugged and white workmen treated the Chinese very badly. However, he had some internal issues to overcome before his idea was accepted. His partner Stanford was virulently anti-Chinese and was elected governor of California partially on that basis. Crocker finally won over Stanford as well as other critics who said the Chinese could not handle a real man's job. He simply said, "They built the Great Wall, didn't they?"

The railroad was built and the Chinese turned out to be excellent workers. They did not get drunk, fight or have strikes. Their particular diet of vegetables, rice and seafood was catered to by the railroad. Many of them stayed on and worked with Crocker on other projects, such as Del Monte. It is no wonder the Chinese name for California is Gold Mountain.

While the Big Four were laying track, an enterprising Scottish businessman was absorbing ranchos in Monterey County. David Jacks had amassed tens of thousands of acres in Monterey County by loaning money to land-poor ranchers and then quickly foreclosing on the loans. He will appear later in this story.

The Big Four always kept their non-rail investments in equal shares in the Pacific Improvement Company. Even after their acrimonious split when Crocker left the Central Pacific, they kept this partnership going. Their heirs had different ideas.

Heirs of the Big Four

W.H. Crocker

By the early 1900s all the original owners of the Pacific Improvement Company (PIC) had died. Their heirs were a diverse and litigious lot. They wanted to divide up the assets and go their separate ways.

Crocker was the only one of the Big four to have surviving natural children, and the Crocker family the only one to retain a presence in San Francisco. Stanford had only one son, Leland Jr., who famously died young, and the university was built in his honor. Huntington and Hopkins had no natural heirs, only adopted families.

Crocker had four children, many of whose progeny still live in or near San Francisco and have been integral in the business and the cultural community to this day. The most successful of the four children was W. H. (Will) Crocker. His brother Fred died young, as did Fred's wife. They left three orphaned children who Will looked after. His other brother, George, and sister, Harriet, married Easterners and moved away. Will ("Big Bill") stayed in San Francisco.

William Henry Crocker (1861-1937)

William Henry Crocker was a banker with an eye for very good investments and a knack for spotting promising young men and promoting their ideas. He was also a very civic-minded citizen of San Francisco and we have him to thank for many public enterprises, from the California Academy of Sciences to the Opera House, in addition to his work on the Panama Pacific International Exhibition and many other endeavors. He was a member of the Bohemian Club, a men's club in San Francisco with a summer retreat called Bohemian Grove. It sits on 4000 acres of redwood-studded beauty on the Russian River in Northern California. There are 120 or so camps at the Grove, Will's was the "Land of Happiness." Will was also a president of the Pacific-Union Club and was very active in San Francisco civic affairs.

Emperor Norton
(1819-1880)

He also immersed himself in the folklore of the city. Will Crocker organized a funeral commemoration of Emperor Norton, the slightly mad San Francisco character who proclaimed himself Emperor of the United States and Protector of Mexico and went about issuing decrees and proclamations. He was tolerated by the citizenry, treated well and became a fixture in the city. My favorite proclamation of the Emperor was, "Whoever… shall be heard to utter the abominable word 'Frisco' shall be guilty of high misdemeanor, and shall pay into the Imperial Treasury $25." No true resident or friend of that city ever refers to it as such. Emperor Norton issued his own currency which was accepted at bars and restaurants around the city. He also decreed a bridge should be built from San Francisco to Oakland as well as a tunnel. Those

decrees were eventually honored and there is a continuing effort to change the name of the Oakland Bay Bridge to The Emperor's Bridge.

John McLaren, Will Crocker and C.A. Shurtleff at the gravesite of Emperor Norton 1935

Will married Ethyl Sperry, a Californian from Stockton whose father had made a small fortune in flour mills, banking and land speculation. They had four children: William, Charles, Ethyl and Helen.

Will, a rich man's son, was no dilettante. His banking expertise and keen eye for good men and investments maintained the family fortune for many generations to come. Big Bill was highly regarded in San Francisco. Sam Morse referred to him as the boss.

The Hopkins Heir
Edward Francis Searles

Mary and Mark Hopkins had no natural children. Mary Hopkins took a liking to the son of her longtime housekeeper, a young man named Timothy Nolan, and the couple adopted him. Unfortunately for him, after Mark Hopkins died in 1878, a New York decorator by the name of Edward Francis Searles seduced and married Mary. She was 22 years older and it turned out Searles was gay. After a six-month honeymoon in Europe, Mary announced in a new will that Timothy Nolan Hopkins was no longer her heir and would be replaced by Searles.

Edward Francis Searles (1841-1920)

After Mary's death in 1891, Searles was left with his wife's vast real estate holdings in San Francisco, New York, Great Barrington, and Methuen, Massachusettes, and $21 million. During the remainder of his life he satisfied his love of architecture by building a number of grand structures, frequently in collaboration with architect Henry Vaughan.

He died Aug. 6, 1920, at his residence, Pine Lodge in Methuen, and is entombed in the Searles Mausoleum on the property at Pine Lodge.

He left much of his vast estate to various colleges and the remainder to his "private secretary," who in turn left his fortune to charities.

After the death of his adoptive mother, Timothy Hopkins (nee Nolan) sued Searles for a share of the estate, but lost. The controversy made good fodder for the press. California papers published stories suggesting Searles exploited Mary's interest in spiritualism and falsified records to wrest the estate from her adopted son and to defraud her business partners. Under oath, Searles testified that he had married Mary "...partly out of affection and partly for her money." He later settled on Timothy a "token" amount of three million dollars "to make him go away." Timothy got the contents of the mansion in San Francisco and the San Francisco Art Institute got the building. It was rumored at the time that Searles had a male lover living with him after Mary's death and that Timothy Hopkins used this information to blackmail Searles after losing the court case.

Timothy Hopkins
(1859-1936)

However, the settlement, or blackmail funds, set up Timothy well enough to found the city of Palo Alto, then called University Park. He became a trustee of Stanford University and served on the board until his death.

Searles may have acquired his money in an underhanded manner, but he spent it well. He settled with Timothy Hopkins and then went on to build his castles, endow schools and contribute to several communities. He is well regarded in the East today: word of how he got his money apparently did not travel across the country.

Searles was not really interested in business and had advisors to deal with it. His primary advisor was Thomas Hamlin Hubbard, a retired civil war general with a distinguished career.

The Stanford Heir
and Leland Stanford Jr. University

Leland and Jane Stanford left the vast bulk of their holdings including 25% of the PIC to the university that bore their son's name. Stanford University continued to be investors in the PIC until the company was finally dissolved in 1961. They were passive investors and happily collected the income the properties delivered.

Jane Stanford
(1828-1905)

Jane Stanford made the university her lifetime project after her husband died in 1893. Although she had professional help operating the nascent enterprise (she had no such experience herself), she was very involved in the decision making. In later years this proved to be less valuable and more complicating, especially after her mental stability came into question.

At age 76, she claimed that someone was trying to poison her, with slightly veiled allusions to the President of Stanford, David Starr Jordan, as the culprit. She drank some bottled water in January 1905 in San Francisco and thought it tasted funny. Her maid and secretary each tried it and agreed. The bottle was sent to the lab and supposedly found to have strychnine in it.

To recover from the experience, she sailed to Hawaii. While staying at the Moana Hotel she ordered up some bicarbonate of soda for an upset stomach. Her secretary, Bertha Berner, prepared it. Later that night Jane cried out, "I am so sick…I have been poisoned again." She died later that evening. Possibly she was not imagining this threat, but the only person present in both cases was her long-time and very loyal secretary.

An autopsy was performed and the conclusion was that Jane had been poisoned by strychnine. David Starr Jordan of Stanford was on his way to Hawaii to meet with her and arrived after she died. He immediately hired a doctor to review the autopsy. This doctor claimed it was natural causes, a heart attack. Jordan put out a press release saying as much and that is still the official story.

The Huntington Heir

When Collis Huntington died childless in 1900, his widow, Arabella (Belle Duval Huntington), married his nephew, Henry E. Huntington. Henry was wealthy in his own right, having worked on the Central Pacific and created Newport News shipbuilding. They moved to Los Angeles after the 1906 earthquake and fire destroyed their home on Nob Hill. Their legacy includes the famous Huntington Library and Gardens and Huntington Beach.

Belle died in 1921. She had already sold her interest in the PIC to Edward Searles. She left her remaining fortune to her son from a prior marriage and Collis's stepson, Archer Milton Huntington. The childless Archer gave most everything he inherited to art museums around the world, founded the Hispanic Society in New York to honor his Latina wife, and a sculpture museum in Virginia as well as other art institutions.

So, by early 1900 the PIC was owned by a gay New York decorator, an aloof university with a meddlesome sole trustee, and the Crocker family, represented by W. H.

(Will) Crocker. The manager of the PIC, A.D. Shepard, had been selected by Searles. By 1915 Shepard had sold off most of the PIC's land and assets although it still owned a large portion of Alameda Island in San Francisco Bay, Castle Crags, Hope Ranch, and many other assets like oil leases in Louisiana and a carbon mine in Washington State. There were a total of 16 corporations and none of them making money, including the crown jewel of the PIC, Del Monte.

Belle Huntington (1821-1924)

Chapter Eight

Del Monte

If John Steinbeck, another Monterey County local, had written about Del Monte instead of Cannery Row, he might've said: "Del Monte was a painting, a dream, a noisy train, a coastline, a playground, a sporting event, a car tour, a cypress tree, a rocky shoreline and a way of life."

Will Crocker met with Sam on his visit to the World's Fair in 1915. He had a new assignment for his protégé: Sam continued to oversee the Crocker-Huffman ranch (for another 21 years) but he would no longer be the onsite manager. Crocker was delighted with the turnaround at the ranch. Although new to the business, Sam simply knew how to do things right. He made the place profitable and efficient. He saw what was needed and had the force of character to get it done. The new assignment turned out to be the last job Sam ever undertook as an employee.

Crocker wanted Sam to be manager of the Pacific Improvement Company. His mission was to liquidate all the PIC properties and distribute the proceeds to the heirs, including the Hotel Del Monte and the related land holdings in Monterey County. The hotel had been Charles Crocker's dream, and his son Will was sad to see it go, but the other owners wanted out, so it had to be done.

Sam happily accepted the offer.

He was 29 years old and running a company with 1,000+ employees with operations spread over California and beyond. The businesses included mines, oil wells, hotels, land developments and ranches. Sam was to liquidate everything including the Hotel Del Monte and related lands and businesses.

Del Monte included a nascent town, a large resort hotel complex, a water company and thousands of acres of undeveloped land. You arrived from San Francisco on the Del Monte Express train and were met at the station by a special coach to the front door of the nearby hotel. In 1915, it was the dream of one man long dead and another man about to enter the picture. Now all that had to be sold, but first it was Sam's job to make it work, make it profitable, and to regain the luster it once had. It was truly a job only someone with Sam's imagination could conceive.

Sam had stayed at the hotel and knew a bit about the lands that came with it. He did not know the history of the area or the PIC and Sheppard's plans, but he set about the business of learning that history, the plans and the current operation immediately.

The hotel was only the beginning of the story. The land that came with it, the Monterey Peninsula, truly fascinated him -- the beautiful rugged coastline, white sand beaches, hills covered in pines and oaks and weather-beaten Monterey Cypress trees. Nearby the Carmel River flowed directly into the Pacific under the gaze of the Mission San Carlos Borroméo de Carmelo, headquarters of the 21 Spanish missions built in the mid 18th century and the home and burial site of the chief cleric, Father (later Saint) Junípero Serra.

Hotel Del Monte, c. 1900 (colorized photo)

Monterey History

Before the hotel was built in 1880 Monterey was a sleepy village of white-washed adobes having seen better days. The sparsely populated town was once famous for its excellent equestrians, but that too was behind it. At one time, it was the most important town of Spanish Alta California: the capital and also the largest town. That changed in 1848 when gold was discovered and the population deserted. This hurt the ranchos most of all: what hired hand would want to work for less than a dollar a day when he could go to the goldfields and make a fortune?

Monterey languished until the hotel was built. This quiet period made recluses like Robert Louis Stevenson happy. Other inhabitants included the Chinese fisherman in the sleepy village of Monterey, who seemed not to care about the gold. The remaining population consisted of a few ranch owners (who had lost their help to the goldfields) and a few struggling merchants, which made it easy pickings for some crafty business-men, most notorious among them a man named David Jacks.

David Jacks

A mong those arriving in California during the Gold Rush was a cunning entrepreneur named David Jacks. Born in Scotland in 1822, Jacks immigrated to New York in 1841 before moving on to California. He prudently invested his savings in revolvers, which he sold at considerable profit in San Francisco. In 1850, Jacks visited Monterey and decided to settle there. During the early 1850s, he worked as an assistant to several Monterey merchants, becoming familiar with the vagaries of local business.

The biggest issue then facing Monterey was the legitimization of the town's claims to some 30,000 acres of Pueblo Lands surrounding the settlement. The land had originally been granted by the Spanish Crown, but after the Spanish left and before the treaty of Guadalupe Hidalgo in 1846 when the U.S. took over the state, California was self-governed. The natives called themselves *Californios*.

David Jacks (1822-1909)

The Pueblo of Monterey hired attorney Delos Rodeyn Ashley to defend their claim before the U.S. Land Commission. Ashley was successful and presented the city with a bill for $991.50. Lacking funds, the town passed a resolution to auction the Pueblo Lands in order to pay the fee. The sale was held in February 1859, with the sole bidders comprised of Ashley and David Jacks, who paid slightly more than $1,000 for the entire 30,000 acres. The sale was harshly criticized, and years later it became the subject of legal challenges. The case eventually came before the U.S. Supreme Court in 1903, which ruled in favor of Jacks—who had acquired Ashley's interest in the property.

Jacks realized that many of the area's prominent citizens—often Mexican ranch owners—were land rich but cash poor after the gold rush. Jacks soon used this to his advantage, loaning money to clients with strained finances and then foreclosing on their property. His acquisition of Rancho Pescadero, now Pebble Beach, was also surrounded in controversy and eventually settled in his favor by the U.S. Supreme Court. Jacks aroused much hostility in this process.

R.L. Stevenson, quoting San Francisco orator Denis Kearny, suggested Jacks should be hanged. His children continued to live there and were not blamed for their father's avarice. His son was locally popular and became the mayor of Monterey at the turn of the century. His last living child of nine, Margaret Anna Jacks, died in 1962 and left her fortune to Stanford University.

Charles Crocker, acting for the Pacific Improvement Company, bought the hotel site and vast tracts of land, but Jacks deeded some of the property to his daughters, and they retained the 1,200 prime acres of Rancho Aguajito near the future hotel. They leased a portion of their land to Crocker to build the Del Monte Golf Course, the oldest continually operating course in the West. Sam tried hard but was initially unable to buy this land. It took over 20 years and lots of haggling to finally wrest it from them.

Crocker had a dream of the grandest seaside resort hotel in the United States, and he would build it on that site. He personally selected the location after a complete tour of the area. The story goes that he toured the Monterey Peninsula with 20 or so guests. It was an early morning in June when they set out and the Peninsula was foggy and chilly as they toured Pebble Beach and Carmel. When they returned to Monterey the sun broke out and they stopped at a small hill looking out over the bay. Crocker's servants spread out a picnic lunch with all sorts of meat, bottles of wine and desserts. It was a glorious afternoon. After the picnic, Crocker stood up, grandly planted his cane in the ground, and said, "We'll build the hotel here." He loved his creation and it became one of the grandest hotels in the world, just as he intended.

The Hotel Del Monte was completed in 1880. It was an immediate sensation, the first luxury seaside destination resort in the country, if not the world. Built in a Victorian style, the hotel had a grand entrance hall, a large dining room and other common areas on 160 acres of manicured gardens including a maze and a large lake with a fountain in the middle. A large swimming pavilion near the beach had a pool with heated salt water and a separate pool for children.

Nearby a private 8,000-acre park called the Del Monte Forest was reserved for hotel guests for picnics and touring. The hotel also included a lodge in nearby Carmel Valley where guests rode, hunted, and explored the trails. Crocker renamed it Rancho Del Monte, but that name never stuck and it reverted to its original Rancho Los Laureles.

The well water near the hotel was brackish and not fit for drinking so Crocker's men searched for a better supply. The Carmel River was on the other side of the hills but supplied fresh clean water year around so he methodically bought up land and water rights in the valley until he controlled it. His workers built an earthen dam about 15 miles up from the ocean just below San Clemente Creek and piped the water into a reservoir on the hills above Monterey. The pipe consisted of a redwood box construction covered in tar and wrapped in canvas.

The Hotel Del Monte, considered one of the finest hotels in America, was extremely popular. In the first few years after it opened, over 3,000 attempted reservations were declined at the fully booked hotel. The grandeur of the place also attracted wealthy folks to buy property and build vacation homes nearby.

The original hotel burned down in 1887 but was quickly rebuilt with two additional wings for guest rooms, expanding the capacity to 450 rooms. It burned again in 1924 during the Morse era, who rebuilt it in a Spanish style.

Hotel Del Monte, as rebuilt by Sam after the 1924 fire

In its first heyday in the late 1800s, the Hotel Del Monte was a bustling end-destination resort. Guests took part in a variety of activities from archery to picnics and, of course, golf, tennis, polo and swimming. A common day might include a drive for a picnic out to the Lodge in Pebble Beach, built in 1909: round trip, 17 miles. The midway point was marked by the Lone Cypress and just beyond, the Pebble Beach Lodge. Originally there were no guest rooms, but a kitchen served lunch to the visitors. The name for the drive continued even after the hotel closed and today people pay $10 to get into Pebble Beach and take The 17 Mile Drive. It winds past grand estates, world-class golf courses, private clubs and luxury guest facilities with the blue Pacific its backdrop. Locals refer to it as The Drive.

It was an obligatory California stop for actors, politicians and the well-to-do and many famous people stayed at the Hotel Del Monte, including Presidents Hayes, Harrison, McKinley and Teddy Roosevelt, the Vanderbilts, the Duke of Alba, Charlie Chaplin, Jean Harlow (who skinny dipped in the Roman Plunge), Salvador Dali and others.

One notable person was dead set against the hotel at the outset. Robert Louis Stevenson lived in Monterey in 1880 and wrote part of his novel *Treasure Island* there. He also wrote descriptive travel articles about the place. He worried (quite rightly) that a "great caravansary" would destroy the idyllic peace of the place. Monterey was once the bustling capital of California, but post gold rush it became a backwater.

Stevenson may have liked this, but development was inevitable as California grew. The land was just too attractive to be ignored.

I was curious about the name Del Monte; Crocker himself gave it the moniker, but why? Del Monte means "from the mountain" in Spanish, but there are no mountains in Monterey. The common story is that he thought it meant from the grove (of trees). No one dared to correct him.

I have a different theory. He hired and imported thousands of Chinese laborers to build his railroad and they also constructed Del Monte and the dam in Carmel Valley. I believe he appropriated it from the Chinese name for California, Gold Mountain. Gold Mountain, from where his own wealth came. Naming the hotel "From the Mountain" would occur to him. Certainly, Gold Mountain was the foundation of his wealth and Del Monte became his legacy.

A side note: the currently well-known food company of the same name supplied a special coffee blend stamped Del

The Lone Cypress

Monte, shipped only to the hotel. They also produced other canned goods with the Del Monte name. In 1891 they asked for permission to adopt the name Del Monte Foods.

The old hotel was the social center for the residents of the area until the advent of World War II. Afterward the communities on the Peninsula became more centric. Monterey, Pacific Grove and Carmel had their own loyal following while Pebble Beach developed an entirely different ambience. The Lodge became the new social center, but the gates into the Del Monte Forest stood as barriers to many.

Southern Pacific

As part of the of building process, Crocker extended his Southern Pacific railway line to Monterey from San Francisco. The hotel had a special train serving it, the Del Monte Express, running directly from San Francisco to Monterey with the first stop at the Del Monte Hotel. This greatly aided the guest count. Many Easterners came to California and were anxious to see the West, thanks to stories by Mark Twain and Bret Harte, as well as paintings by Bierstadt, Russell and others. The transcontinental railroad took about two weeks to cross the country over millions of acres of unspoiled lands and roving bands of hostile Indians. The tourists arrived in San Francisco, spent a few days in the city and then took a convenient four-hour train ride to Monterey, instead of two or three days by carriage.

After the San Francisco earthquake in 1906, a year that preceded a national financial panic, hotel visits declined. The graceful lady that was Del Monte no longer attracted the crowds she once commanded, due not only to economic conditions but also the management style. As Sam Morse pointed out years later, the place needed an owner operator. After the death of the founder, Charles Crocker (who never fully recovered from a carriage accident in New York and died at the Hotel Del Monte in 1888) a series of hired managers ran the operation but there was no principal player interested in it. It had clearly been Charles Crocker's baby.

Chapter Nine

Enter "The Boss"

Charles Crocker's son, Will Crocker, was dissatisfied with what was going on at the Pacific Improvement Company. Every operation was losing money and the sale of assets moved slowly and erratically. He wanted new management and got the Stanford Trustees to side with him. Searles, who controlled 50 percent of the PIC, was not interested in the tawdry life of a businessman. He did not put up much of an argument. His primary advisor, General Hubbard, ran his affairs and the general's man at the PIC, A.D. Sheppard, ran the PIC.

The heirs fired Sheppard as manager of the PIC and hired Sam. General Hubbard felt railroaded and made Sam's life as hellish as possible for a while. They ended up on good terms and the general returned to New York where he died shortly thereafter.

In his memoirs, Sam said about the PIC that he fell heir to a vast collection of businesses with nothing making any money. In 1914, the PIC had to borrow money to pay taxes. In his review of the assets of the PIC there were two glaring money losers: the old El Carmelo Hotel in Pacific Grove and the mining operations in Carbonado, Washington.

Pacific Grove

The El Carmelo was built in 1887 by the company, opening just before the Hotel Del Monte was destroyed by fire. It later served as an inexpensive alternative. It was never very profitable, most likely because they could not serve liquor in the dry town of Pacific Grove. When Sam arrived, it had been losing money for years and he offered to sell it to the city. He told them if they didn't want it he would demolish it. They didn't think he was serious and didn't respond, hoping he would continue to operate it. He promptly took the hotel apart and used the beautiful seasoned lumber two years later to rebuild the Del Monte Lodge, which conveniently burned down in 1917. This was Sam's first battle with the church town.

The PIC owned most all of Pacific Grove except for a portion of the town proper, which Jacks had founded. Originally it was a tent camp on land leased from Jacks for summer chautauquas run by the Methodist Church. The town developed with small lots and the owners eventually built houses. People came from the Bay Area to enjoy the chautauqua and many stayed.

By the time Sam arrived on the scene, much of Pacific Grove had already been developed with tents pitched on small lots. However, the land was undeveloped near the lighthouse. He sold all the remaining small lots in the town in one auction, and focused on the area he called Pacific Grove Acres, noted for its sylvan landscape and meandering contoured roads. In 1932 he built a nine hole golf course near the lighthouse and offered to sell it to the city for a a token payment and a promise that the city would maintain and water the course for five years. After the company built the golf course they were able to sell higher priced lots around it. This was left to the manager of the Pacific Grove Department of the PIC, Charlie Wilson, who Sam held in high regard. He sold the site of the former El Carmelo to W.R. Holman, whose department store served the Peninsula well for many years. Holman had ambitions, one of which put him in direct confrontation with Sam.

The U.S. Army's Presidio of Monterey separated Pacific Grove from old Monterey, which worried Holman. He feared the presidio might close "in case of trouble" and then cut off his access to the main highway. (This is actually the case now as it and most all army bases restricted access after 9/11.) He wanted the county to open up the 17 Mile Drive as a secondary route. This was anathema to Sam: it would ruin his image of the Peninsula. Del Monte Forest was and is a gated community, giving it an exclusive nature besides being a good source of revenue for road maintenance. Holman was determined and found some obscure law about connecting potentially landlocked cities of a certain size with a highway. Holman went to the county Board of Supervisors where the president, L.D. Roberts, told him no highway would be built while he was in office. Holman then set out on a successful drive to block Roberts' reelection and threatened to block county bond issues if the funds for the highway were not included.

At some point, Sam met with Holman, and they agreed to a compromise. Holman could have his highway, but it would be over the hill and not through Pebble Beach proper. They had it put in its current location, up in the hills through Del Monte Forest, but away from the sports area. It is known as The Holman Highway or Highway 68.

Carbonado

The PIC owned 78 town sites as a result of the railroad construction and Sam's job was to dispose of them in one way or another. One interesting site was Carbonado, a company town in Washington State. The centerpiece was the very productive Carbon Hill Mine and the company owned the town – including all the buildings, homes and businesses. On his first trip to inspect the property, a very ugly and intense strike was happening at the mine. The operators had dealt with the strike by hiring veterans just back from the war in 1918: young men hungry for work and terribly resented by the strikers. One poor old woman had a heart attack and died when strikers burned her son, the foreman, in effigy on her front lawn.

The mine boss greeted Sam at the railway station in Carbonado and they drove out to the mine. The mine boss had a gun in his lap and gave one to Sam advising him that things might get ugly. When they drove through the strikers, people pounded on the car and yelled but nothing worse happened. They arrived at the mine safely and went on to inspect it. Carbon had been in big demand, but the mine appeared to be nearing the end of its productive life. Sam found a buyer for the mine quickly, but no one wanted to buy the town, which they eventually gave to the occupants after the mine closed.

Del Monte 1915

When they lived in Visalia and Merced Sam and Anne and their three kids went often to Monterey to get out of the oppressive heat of the Central Valley. They would stay at the grand old Hotel Del Monte when they felt they could afford it or the Pacific Grove Hotel, the less expensive alternative. Their initial trip was in June 1908 when their first child (Sam Jr.) was only a month old. This summer, and again when their second child was born, they rented a house in Pacific Grove. It was also in 1908 when Sam first met W.H. Crocker while on a picnic. The hot summers in Visalia were no place for the new mother and her infant child. After that first trip the family continued to migrate to foggy Monterey.

They fell in love with the place. The weather, the coastline and the good life of Monterey was very appealing. They knew the PIC owned the hotels, but had no idea that Sam would be running them a few years later.

After the earthquake and fire devastated San Francisco and the panic of 1907 swept through Wall Street, guest nights fell off considerably at the hotels. The Del Monte coped with this by laying off staff and reducing services. Although this worked in the short term, the quality of their guests declined and revenue soon followed.

When Sam came down as manager and liquidator of the Pacific Improvement Company, he arrived on the Del Monte Express. On his first inspection of the property, he was greeted and given a tour by the hotel manager, H. R. Warner, an A.D. Sheppard hire. As they walked around the place Sam asked questions and made suggestions, but each time came the same reply, "That is not the way we do things here." Finally fed up with this intractable fellow Sam pointed out that "the way we do things" was not working so well, and that is why he was there. In his memoirs, Sam recalled the next part of the conversation.

"I then said to him as follows, 'Either I have got to find a manager who believes the operation can be changed and the place can make money, or I have got to tear it down, because it is my business to cut losses and convert useless property into money if I can do it.'"

The manager caught the next train to San Francisco and went right to see W.H. Crocker. He complained that he knew the business and should be in charge, not some Yale cowboy, but Crocker stood by his decision and stuck with Sam. Much of the staff left with Warner. The head clerk, Walter Houston, also gave notice, but kindly waited until a new manager was in place. It was 1915 and the World's Fair was going on and the hotel expected a lot of business. It was a tough situation for Sam.

A friend asked him if he had heard of Carl Stanley. Sam knew him from a stay in a San Diego hotel several years earlier. His friend said Stanley was running the Clark Hotel in Stockton but might be interested in a better situation. Sam and his friend went to Stockton and looked him up.

Carl Stanley was just as Sam remembered him -- well groomed, soft spoken and the very picture of the competent hotel manager. Sam asked him to come to his San Francisco office the next Monday and Stanley accepted Sam's offer to run the hotel.

Sam's only advice to Stanley was that the place should be run more like a club than hotel: keep out undesirables and let the guests have free use of the place. Stanley ran the hotel for the next 27 years until the building was turned over to the Navy. He found an excellent chef, Jean Julliard, as well as a crew of clerks, and soon the place was fully staffed. Sam and Stanley installed a grill for more casual dining, introduced dancing and allowed smoking in the main dining room. The activity alone reinvigorated the staff and Sam's timing could not have been better. The World's Fair opened in San Francisco just as he was taking over Del Monte. Needless to say, this helped bring business to Monterey on the Del Monte Express.

There was more to be done to get the property ready for sale: an expensive undertaking as the infrastructure was negligible. But Sam convinced Crocker the upgrades were worth it.

One of the first projects was water. Sam commissioned a new dam built on the Carmel River, the best source of water for the area. Wells in Monterey produced water with a brackish taste due to their proximity to the ocean and the next closest river was the Salinas, which also had salinity problems. Charles Crocker secured the water rights by buying up property in Carmel Valley. On the Carmel there was an old earthen dam referred to as the Chinese Dam, named for Crocker's Chinese laborers. It was small and unsafe.

The new dam, upstream from the old one, was placed where the San Clemente Creek joined the Carmel River. The water was piped to a reservoir called Forest Lake in the Del Monte Forest and from there distributed to the hotel as well as to the people of Monterey, Pacific Grove and eventually Carmel. Sam named the company the Monterey Water Works.

The Pebble Beach Lodge, c. 1922

Sam also dreamed about the future of Pebble Beach. At that time, there were three or four log cabins and the old log Lodge. The Chinese fishing village on Stillwater Cove had burned down and the lease not renewed. The northern part of the Peninsula was mostly sand dunes, swamp and a dense pine forest.

Sam felt the future of the company was Pebble Beach and developing home sites for the wealthy. The first step was to add guest rooms at the lodge. The twenty rooms were called Cottage Row. The second, tear up Sheppard's development map with all the tiny lots cramming more than 400 sites along the ocean and inland, the 6th -13th fairways of the current Pebble Beach Golf Links. Sam bought back the lots that were sold but not built on. His investors grumbled about a slower pace of return but were eventually convinced. Only one man refused, no matter how good the offer. He was so adamant he put a restriction on the property that it would never be sold to Del Monte. Years later new owners worked around the restriction by giving a portion of the land closest to the sea to the company in exchange for adjacent land further inland. The company rerouted the fifth hole of the golf course on their new property, thus completing Sam's vision.

The infrastructure was set up and construction began. Next, entice people to the hotel and sell them lots. Monterey was a backwater in the early 1900s and the Pebble Beach sports area was undeveloped. I asked Boss what people did there at that time and he said one of the favorite things was a picnic. The hotel packed lunches, guests piled into a carriage (and later cars) and drove to one of the idyllic nearby spots, the old Lodge in Pebble Beach a favorite. There were only a few houses in Pebble Beach and the ride was through beautiful sylvan countryside with breathtaking views of the Pacific. The carriages stopped at the Lodge and the guests enjoyed the view with their picnic.

This section of the California coastline was not yet described as "the greatest meeting of land and sea," but people marveled at the beauty of the old pine forest, the glorious coastline, the Lone Cypress, the quaint pueblos of old Monterey, the big farms just inland, and the muscular cliffs of Big Sur which were only accessible by horseback until 1933. The old Carmel Mission was being restored and two San Francisco lawyers, James Frank Devendorf and Frank Powers, were building an artist colony in Carmel.

The Hotel Del Monte was the central social gathering point for many of the local residents. Recently, William Zellerbach, one of the few people I've met who stayed at the hotel in the 30s, told me a story just before he passed away at age 97. He described a wonderful evening he experienced as a young man in the old hotel: they danced and dined all evening and he smoked his first cigarette. Maybe other firsts too, there was a twinkle in his eye, but we met at a gentlemen's club and explored no further.

Sam made sure his guests enjoyed their visit, but he also wanted them to come back to settle there. The hotel was an integral part of his vision for the Peninsula, but there was a lot to be done first. He never doubted himself or let fear slow him down. Sometimes this got him in trouble and fistfights, but generally it was the right course of action. Sam has been described as a man with limitless energy who could "out imagine anyone."

The Early Years

Sam and his family initially settled in Hillsborough and Sam took the Del Monte Express down to Monterey when he needed to, usually by himself. He stayed at the hotel and later the company built him a house adjacent to the Lodge on the 18th fairway. The commute was pleasant enough. He usually left in the morning, stayed a day or two and went back to San Francisco where he had an office in the Crocker Building at One Montgomery Street. (This was the same location for my first job 60 years later in 1975. Amusingly, the job offer came from Charles Crocker III, grandson of W.H. Crocker, my grandfather's mentor. I didn't take the train.)

On one memorable train ride to Monterey during prohibition, Sam ran into W.W. (Bill) Crocker, Will's son, and Templeton's cousin. The two enjoyed "Oliver's excellent martinis" on the Del Monte Express and arrived at the hotel in very good moods. (Prohibition must have taken a rear berth to indulgence on the Del Monte.) Sam suggested Bill have a party in his new beautiful house in Pebble Beach, "Villa Amici." Crocker agreed, and when they arrived at the Hotel Del Monte, Crocker announced to Mr. Stanley, the manager, that he was having a party at his house that night and asked him to send over an orchestra and champagne.

Sam and Bill went to the Grill Room where they met friends and had dinner. The Grill was a big success. By this time the crowd was just as affluent as before but much less stuffy. Guests wanted to have fun in a much more active way. They were also opening their minds to new ideas and associations as well. Del Monte was a suitable venue to meet those criteria.

The evening was splendid, the wine flowing and at the end of the dinner Bill Crocker invited the group back to his house for a final-final. When they arrived at his house, all were surprised to see lights blazing, music emanating from the ball-room and servants ready to take their coats. Sam and Bill completely forgot they had asked Mr. Stanley to set up a party. They split the champagne with the orchestra, sent the waiters home and continued to enjoy themselves. Sam said it was no problem to have a night of revelry and still be ready for business in the morning: a big hearty breakfast and a little exercise and you would be ready for the day.

During these early years in Monterey, Sam and Anne were having trouble in their marriage. Sam was always on the go and often away from home. There were rumors of other women. Anne was a devout Christian Scientist and most likely refused to put up with Sam's lifestyle. They split up in 1916 and divorced in 1918. She took their three children, Sammy, Jack, and Nancy to Chicago where she soon married George Richardson, the trustee of the Marshall Fields estate. Sam stayed on and began spending more time in Monterey. Many important people were coming to the hotel, including presidents.

Teddy Roosevelt

Before Sam's time, Presidents Harrison, Hayes, McKinley and Teddy Roosevelt had stayed at Del Monte. Sam admired Teddy greatly, although likely did not agree with some of his more progressive ideas. Teddy was the original conservationist and was extremely popular at the turn of the last century when Sam was a teenager. Sam adopted this philosophy and felt his primary goal was to conserve the lands he acquired. He has been called an early environmentalist but that was too extreme for him. He was a conservationist who wanted to fit humans and their habitation into the environment.

He met Teddy in 1915 in San Francisco when Teddy, by now out of office, was gearing up for WWI. Teddy was familiar with Del Monte and stayed there during his presidency. He is pictured on a horse in front of the hotel. After the picture was taken, Teddy took off by himself and rode through the forest. No one saw him for hours and it drove his security crazy. Sam says of meeting him, "Anyone who ever met the famous Teddy experienced an impact they would likely not forget as long as they retained their mentality. He was a dynamo…the kind of man I admired tremendously."

Roosevelt was forming a unit of Rough Riders to fight in the upcoming war and asked Sam to join. Sam was elated and immediately said yes. The War Department turned down the former president's idea of his own brigade, but several of the men who volunteered formed a group called "The Grizzlies." Sam did not join. He tried to volunteer in 1916 but was turned down during the physical. He thought he was in perfect shape and he looked it, but the doctor saw his major surgery scars, the aftermath of his 1910 trip to Mexico when he contracted amoebic dysentery and appendicitis. He had three separate operations in just over two weeks. Sam said of that experience, "At one time I had six drains in my body, but apparently I recovered." His recovery was insufficient to qualify for the U.S. Army. He did however, join the Citizen Cavalry at the Presidio of San Francisco.

With a letter written on his behalf by Teddy to the Army, Sam finally got an appointment in 1918 with the rank of Captain of Engineers, but got no further than New York when the armistice was declared. He related that the party in New York City was unforgettable: no car or bus traffic, the streets filled with people walking, laughing and joking and torn bits of paper flying through the air.

Chapter Ten

Pebble Beach

In the late 1910s Sam was busy spending the PIC money, improving Del Monte and preparing it for sale. The new Lodge and golf course in the sports area (Pebble Beach) were on track for a 1918 completion and big beautiful homes were being built. The Newport of the West was taking shape. Of course, the Crockers had first pick and selected lots near the Ghost Tree on the southwest corner of the Peninsula. Other well-known, wealthy socialites who stayed at the old hotel wanted homes there – the Tobins, the Irwins, William Garland from Los Angeles, and Louis Hill, all built large showplaces still there today, one still owned by a Crocker.

This time, The Del Monte Lodge was rebuilt with guest rooms. The golf course, designed by Jack Neville, was expanded from 9 to 18 holes. Jack was a top-ranked amateur but never designed a golf course before or after. He had a made-to-order palette with which to work. Eliminating the small lots allowed him to build a classic links course along the ocean front. Sam got in the act later and personally redesigned the 18th hole, turning it into a par five. This upgrade in Pebble Beach was designed to attract a higher price from potential purchasers.

Amid all the dramatic changes in the U.S. in 1918 (soldiers returning from the war, the Spanish Flu, the advent of Prohibition, politicians gearing up to gain women's votes) Sam found a buyer for the hotel and properties, G. W. Herkschier, an old friend from Yale.

There was a catch though. They wanted to keep Sam as manager but did not want to include him in the ownership. This was not acceptable to him. He knew the operation had to be owner occupied to be successful. However he now had a fair price ($1,300,000) for the properties, and he planned to use that in negotiations with the Crockers.

Sam, enjoying his new position as the dominant force on the Monterey Peninsula, was abruptly reminded of his purpose there one Friday afternoon late in 1918. Sam was riding his horse, Moonlight, around Pebble Beach dreaming of future years when a rider approached him on the trail.

"I am glad I found you, Mr. Morse," said the young man. Recognizing one of his clerks, Sam asked what he needed. "Mr. Crocker is arriving on the afternoon Express to meet with you." Sam galloped back to the hotel to prepare for the meeting.

Despite his good work at the hotel and its improving profit stream, the Crocker family and the other heirs were still anxious to sell all the PIC holdings and liquidate the partnership. (As it turns out, it took until 1961 to finally wrap it up, 43 years later.)

When Will Crocker arrived at Del Monte that day with his nephew Templeton in tow, Sam presented his plan. First, he reviewed the hotel operations and the progress of the forest area development. He brought them up to date on the golf course, new Lodge, and the big dam construction in Carmel Valley and the valuable water rights to the Carmel River. They discussed the effect of the upcoming Constitutional Amendment soon to be known as Prohibition. They wondered how the hotel and restaurants would do without liquor. "The Noble Experiment" was set to be enacted in 1919. The thought of Prohibition made the Crockers even more anxious to sell.

Sam brought up the offer from the East Coast group to the Crockers and then hit them with the bombshell: he would match this very fair offer himself. He said it was obvious to him that to be really successful long term the place needed an owner-operator. He believed he was the best possible choice to be the owner and the operator.

There was one major sticking point: he needed the Crockers. The offer for the property was for $1.3 million and Sam did not have that kind of money. He had saved some over the last few years but nowhere near the amount required. The initial stake inherited from his father had been depleted by his illness in 1910. The costs of rearing a family in the right style also took its toll. He devised a plan to raise the money with Herbert Fleishhacker of the Anglo Bank in San Francisco through a bond offering. He asked the Crockers, who did have that kind of money and more, if they would purchase the entire offering, basically underwriting the sale. The Crockers said they would review the offer and let him know.

He did not know of the people in the Crocker offices who didn't want him to succeed. Paul Fagan, a senior officer in the organization, did not trust Sam. He was perhaps jealous of the attention Sam received from Crocker. C. B. Alexander, Will's sister Harriet Crocker's husband, was also was concerned that the operation would never be profitable. Not knowing this, Sam pressed on with the plan.

Three weeks later he received a letter from W.H. declining to invest. Crocker told Sam that Templeton, C.B. (Alexander) and he had lunch at the University Club in San Francisco and discussed the matter. They felt they should not loan the money because "they did not want to be both a buyer and a seller on the same transaction."

Sam was devastated. He had convinced himself Crocker would help. On top of that Sam had just received the news that his mother was ill and would soon pass away. He knew if someone else bought the place and started giving orders, he would not be able to stay there and complete his "painting." He wanted to be the one running the show. Sam had recently remarried and tried to explain this to his new wife, Relda. He was resolute about this, but all Relda saw was that her newly-wedded husband might be looking for job.

The University Club
Fifth Avenue & 54th Street

My dear Sam —

Templeton, C. B. A, and I lunched together a few days ago and we took up several matters for discussion and decision. A night letter was sent covering several of the decisions that we reached. The Del Monte properties project was discussed and Mr. Alexander stated that he had referred the offer, made to me in your several letters, to the different members of his family. They do not, he says, care to invest. Templeton stated that he likewise does not care to invest and it is due you to know that I likewise do not wish to continue as an owner in the property. It is not consistent for me to be both a vendor and purchaser —

I have no doubt you will make a great success and I very much hope that you will —

Yours very truly
Wm. H. Crocker —

Sunday. March 23rd 1919. —

W. H. Crocker's 1919 letter to Sam declining to invest
"It is not consistent for me to be both a vendor and a purchaser."

Sam did not know what happened to cause the Crockers to lose faith in him, but he did not give up. Whatever the problem, he would take the refusal at face value and move on. That was Sam's old football training -- learn how to fall so you can get right back up again. When he lost a battle, whether it was with Holman over the proposed highway through Pebble Beach or the redevelopment plan for Monterey, he took it in stride and just assumed the other side would eventually suffer from their mistake. He had no self-doubt. In the end, Crocker showed he still had some faith in Sam and kept him on as head of the PIC.

The hunt was on for the money. He called on San Francisco banks, but in 1919 money was still tight, and at first no one was interested in making the loan. Banker Herbert Fleishhacker, however, had an interesting proposition.

Herbert Fleishhacker (1872-1957)

Fleishhacker was the head of the Anglo Bank and 1918 had been a good year. His bank was doing well. He had just completed a major financing in Seattle, details of which would come back to haunt him in later years, but at that moment he had cash few others had. He offered to be Sam's partner and take care of the financing. Sam liked Herbert, but he didn't want a partner.

Eventually Fleishhacker won Sam over by convincing him he would not interfere with operations or Sam's plans to develop Pebble Beach. He slightly modified this when development actually started by insisting on deed restrictions excluding Asians, Africans or people under the subjection of the former Ottoman Empire, meaning Arabs and Jews. The family story is he did not want his own sons buying houses there as he feared it would lower property values. Somewhat oblivious to or more likely agreeing with this obvious racism, Sam agreed to it. It was not until 1963 that his son-in-law, my father Richard Osborne, then president of the company, had the offensive language removed.

Sam and Herbert became good friends and remained so until Herbert died in 1957. He was on the board and a major partner until 1938 when he filed for bankruptcy, and Sam bought him out but kept him on the board.

Sam and Herbert Fleishhacker, c. 1930

Herbert and Sam made the deal with Crocker: Herbert would pay the PIC the $1.3 million cash with loans arranged from his bank. After that deal was done and the PIC paid, they raised additional funds with a bond offering of $1,000,000 to repay the short term loans and have working capital.

Del Monte Properties

S am and Herbert created a holding company called Del Monte Properties (DMP) with Sam as president and Herbert vice-president. The board consisted of San Francisco businessmen including oilman K.R. Kingsbury, attorney Hugh Goodfellow, ship-builder Henry Scott, developer of Hope Ranch and classmate of Sam's at Yale, Maurice Heckscher, and Charles W. Clark, miner and married to banking heiress Celia Tobin. These men plus Sam and Herb were the first directors. Notably absent were members of the Crocker family or officers of the Crocker Bank.

The acquisition of the Hotel Del Monte included vast acreage on the desirable Monterey Peninsula as well as large tracts of land in Carmel Valley along the Carmel River. This valley property was bought primarily for the water rights and almost immediately put up for sale while retaining 1,000 acres around the dam and the pipes that brought the water to the Peninsula.

San Clemente Dam and the Monterey Water Works

T he Monterey Water Works (MWW) supplied water for much of the Monterey Peninsula at the time and continues today under the current ownership of Cal-Am. The water came from the Carmel River from a dam constructed about 20 miles upstream, a simple earthen dam locals referred to as the Chinese Dam. This dam was never meant to be permanent and was one of the many of Sam's deferred improvements. He built a reinforced concrete dam where the San Clemente Creek joined the Carmel River. He was very proud of the dam, completed in 1920.

Although Sam estimated it would be good for 50 years, the new owners operated it until 2010. It was demolished in 2015 at a cost of $80,000,000, the biggest ever dam removal in the state of California.

The Monterey Water Works proved to be a good asset for Del Monte Properties Company. It provided, pardon me, a steady stream of income, and as the Peninsula grew so did the value of the assets. This was one of two subsidiary companies inside the holdings not directly related to guest services or property sales. The MWW provided water to Monterey, Carmel, Pebble Beach and Pacific Grove, as well as the old hotel. In the early part of the Depression, Sam sold the water company and used the proceeds to keep the hotel and Lodge going. He made several side deals on the sale including free water for his personal properties until 1980. The sale of the water company left the sand plant as the only steady source of revenue.

San Clemente Dam, completed 1920, demolished 2015

Sand Mining

The beaches around the Del Monte Forest have beautiful fine white sand which has many uses. The company built a refining plant on the northern shore of the Peninsula near the huge sand dunes, the present site of the Spanish Bay golf resort. The dunes were still there when I was a child and it was great fun to "ski" down them on cardboard, which we did secretly, since it was forbidden by the company. The danger of being buried by sand-slides was quite real, but we didn't consider that since it was so much fun. My sister Ellen rode her horse down the dunes and said it was a wonderful sensation to slide like that on a big horse.

The sand was washed at the plant and shipped out by a railroad spur built for the purpose. The railroad line hugged the coast around Pacific Grove and ended at the depot in Monterey. As a boy, I rode on one of the last trains out of the sand plant and got to sit up front with the engineer. After the plant closed in the 1950s, Sam gave the railroad right-of-way to the cities of Pacific Grove and Monterey. Today much of it is a well-used bike and footpath. The gift also allowed unimpeded access for pedestrians to the coastline of Monterey Bay.

The sand operation remained a profitable enterprise and helped the company enormously during the Depression. In the mid '60s Del Monte Properties acquired another sand company, Wedron Silica based in Chicago, as a balance against the seasonal operations of the resort. The acquisition was made with stock diluting Sam's ownership but not his control. He continued to call the shots as he had from the beginning in 1915 until he died in 1969.

Del Monte Lodge

The development of the Del Monte Lodge in Pebble Beach started after the fire in 1917 destroyed the old log structure. Sam's vision did not include rustic structures in Pebble Beach and was happy to replace the building. They started to build immediately with the lumber from Hotel El Carmelo in Pacific Grove. Additional guest rooms and a small shopping area were added. The golf course was completed late in 1918 and new roads were laid out and other infrastructure required for development. Meanwhile, the Hotel Del Monte regained its luster and was ready for the "Roaring Twenties."

This was Sam's first heyday. He created the club-like environment at the hotel and everyone wanted to be a member. It was less formal and more inviting and, after the fire in 1924, was rebuilt in the Spanish style Sam preferred instead of the old-fashioned Victorian. Both of my grandfathers were born in the 1880s and shared a dislike for the overly fussy ornate constructions of their youth. Sam loved the history of Monterey and focused on the Spanish heritage. His friend Frank McComas painted a large mural in the lobby of the hotel depicting the arrival of Captain Gaspar de Portolá and Father Junípero Serra in the 1770s claiming the territory for Spain. When the new hotel was completed, Sam invited Spain's Duke of Alba to visit. One of the Duke's many titles was the Count of Monterey, and Monterey, California was named for his direct ancestor.

The real profits were not in the hotel but in developing the property, and there was a lot of property to develop. Sam was very happy and excited about what he had acquired. His home life was also a source of new happiness.

Sam (center) and the Duke of Alba (right)

Chapter Eleven

Relda

About the time Sam was talking to the Crockers about buying Del Monte, he met Relda Ford. After he and Anne split up in 1916, Sam enjoyed life as a bachelor along with his buddy Harry Hunt. Harry was the scion of a wealthy family with a vast liquor business Harry presciently sold in the late 1910s. He was proud to say he never worked a day in his life after that well-timed sale. He enjoyed the good life, playing polo and golf and socializing at Del Monte and in San Francisco. Sam quoted Harry in

Relda Ford Morse (1888-1951)

his memoirs. When asked what he liked about Pebble Beach, Harry replied, "It is just the living there." Harry and Sam were together when they each met their future wives on the same night at the same time.

The story of their meeting, as told to my mother, was that her mother, Relda and her friend, Jane Selby, were entering a charity ball together in San Francisco. They spotted two handsome fellows. Jane said to Relda, "Look at the guy with the gaudy diamond pinky ring and, my goodness, spats! No one has worn them for ages. I'll take him. You can have the big guy." The man in the spats was Harry Hunt and the big guy was Sam. This choice worked out well for everyone.

Relda Ford had just fled her first husband, a man named Stott who, according to family stories, locked her up in their apartment in New York. There is not much lore about him, but clearly good riddance. Jane Atherton Selby had also suffered through a brief marriage. Now they were enjoying the single carefree divorcee life, soon to end.

Jane Selby was a descendant of Faxon Atherton, California pioneer and the Bay Area town's namesake. She traveled in fine circles and counted as her close friends the future Duchess of Windsor, Wallis Simpson, the well-known painter Gene Francis, and many others. Relda's father had been Attorney General of California after entering politics in Downieville, California, his place of birth. Her mother was the daughter of an Irish immigrant who came to California in the 1850s.

Sam and Relda were married for over 30 years until she passed away in 1951. Jane and Harry Hunt also stayed happily married and the two couples were close friends. The Hunts lived on Ondulado Road in Pebble Beach.

(left) Harry Hunt. (right) Mrs. Harry Hunt and Marquessa de Portago and pet goat at polo, 1928.

Sam once described Relda as being "of '49ers stock, which in California is like being descended from the Puritans in New England, but a hell of a lot more fun." Relda was indeed a lot of fun and lived a full but short life.

Relda's grandmother, Mary Catherine Freehill, came to California in the 1850s with her brother and went directly to the gold fields. They came from County Cavan in Ireland. She met her husband, Lewis Byington, in the boomtown of Downieville. He came to California from Ohio seeking riches in the Sierra foothills, but found he could do better selling meat to the miners. I was always told (incorrectly it turns out) that Lewis came in '49 and Catherine in '51. There was an old ditty my mother recited to me that went:

> "The Miners came in '49
> The whores in '51
> And from that holy union
> Came the native son."

When I asked my mother about her great-grandmother she sternly replied, "Catherine came with her brother." Actually, Lewis came in '51 and Catherine in '53. Men substantially outnumbered women in the gold country even in 1853, but not all those women were prostitutes by any means. As children we heard that her brother did well in the goldfields and Catherine was soon married to Byington. They had two children, Lewis Jr., who became a lawyer/politician and Emma, mother of Relda.

Tirey L. Ford

Tirey L. Ford, Relda's father, from Paris, Missouri, near Hannibal, was the son of the local sheriff with the wonderful name of Pleasant Lafayette Ford. Descendants of French Huguenots who came to Virginia in the later 1600s, each generation moved further west. Tirey found his way to California in 1878 and worked on the giant Glenn Ranch in Northern California, now known as Glenn County. Hugh Glenn was an uncle by marriage and recognized Tirey as bright and ambitious. He sent him to study law in Chico then on to Downieville. While in Downieville, he met Emma Byington, and they fell in love and got married there in 1888.

As a lawyer, he got involved in politics. He first ran for and was elected the district attorney for the five counties comprising the gold country. Then he was elected state senator for the area and subsequently became attorney general for the State of California in 1899.

While working as attorney general, Tirey was also a private attorney with clients including Isaias Hellman and other San Francisco financiers. This was acceptable in those days. The dual role, however, was not to his liking and he resigned as attorney general of the state in 1902.

That year, Tirey and Emma moved to San Francisco with their children. After the '06 earthquake he built a large house at 3800 Clay and lived there until the '20s. Tirey continued to work for Hellman and then got involved in the rebuilding of San Francisco after the earthquake of 1906. First, he was on a committee to oversee the reconstruction of the city. This proved not an easy task as Boss Ruef had to approve every project.

Boss Ruef was the San Francisco version of Tammany of New York. He controlled the unions and in effect controlled City Hall. When John Calhoun, president of United Railroads, wanted to install a trolley car line to the new Parkside development in the Sunset district he was planning on overhead wires to power the line. Citizens objected to that as unsightly, and preferred the wires be put underground, a much more expensive undertaking. Calhoun went to Ruef for help on the matter, and hired Tirey Ford as his lawyer. Ford delivered $200,000 in small bills to Ruef for "payment of legal services." The mayor and supervisors soon saw the wisdom of overhead wires and unanimously agreed to allow them. A great hubbub ensued led by Hiram Johnson, the future governor

Tirey Lafayette Ford (1857-1928) 18th attorney general of California and newspaper man William Randolph Hearst. Ruef was arrested and Ford, among others was indicted. During the trial Ruef adamantly defended Ford and said the payment was indeed for legal fees. Ruef went to prison and never again regained his status as kingpin. The charges against Ford were dropped and he resumed his work on the rebuilding of San Francisco.

Tirey must have been infected by Sam's love of local history. After the death of Emma in 1908, and in retirement, he spent time with Sam and Relda in Monterey and got to know the area well. In 1926 he wrote the short history *Dawn and the Dons*, illustrated by Jo Mora, a friend of Sam's and a sculptor and illustrator of some renown. The illustrations add interest as, among other things, Ford's views of the Indians were pretty old-fashioned. The book can be found in collector's bookshops like Shein and Shein in San Francisco and in some libraries.

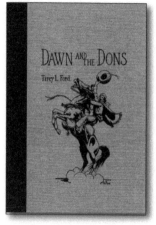

Dawn and The Dons
a history of Monterey
by Tirey L. Ford

In the small-world department, my business partner Ken Berry now owns the house that Tirey and Emma built. He is the second owner after the widower Tirey sold before he moved into the Pacific Union Club, where he died in 1929. The Pacific Union Club eventually banned permanent residents.

Relda and the Other Relda

Tirey made up the name Relda for his daughter and considered it unique. However, one day strolling through San Francisco he noticed an advertisement for a strip joint featuring a dancer named Relda. Intrigued, he went to the performance and went backstage to meet her. He asked how she got the name, the same as his daughter's. The dancer replied, "Oh, that's just my last name, Adler, spelled backwards."

We know of no other Reldas.

The attractive and vivacious Relda, the daughter not the dancer, grew up in San Francisco. Like Sam, one of her parents died when she was just 20. Her mother, Emma Byington Ford, had cancer and passed away quietly in San Francisco. Her Irish grandmother, Catherine, with whom Relda had a strong bond, lived a long life well into the 1920s. She continued to live in Downieville and often visited young Relda.

With a busy father and no mother to provide guidance, Relda was known as a party girl and had an unfortunate early marriage. When the marriage ended in 1915, she returned to San Francisco where she met Sam a couple of years later. Although Relda loved parties and enjoyed people, she was also a very private person. After she met Sam that need for privacy was soon put to the test. Sam has been described as a total extrovert, which was surely tough on Relda. It was a challenge for Sam's first wife, Anne, who complained Sam did not spend enough time with her and the children. He fell back on the excuse that his business was demanding, but the truth was he just damn well did what he enjoyed and what needed doing to make his business work. He wanted to make deals, build things and be in the company of similar-minded men. He also enjoyed the company of other women. This left little time for family and Anne and the children suffered from his lack of attention. This was not the case early in his second marriage.

Sam and Relda were married in a quiet ceremony in Oakland in 1919. It was a second marriage for each of them and Sam was trying to put his deal together to buy Del Monte. There were only a few close friends attending, including Harry and Jane Hunt.

Chapter Twelve

Prohibition

1919 was a pivotal year. The great war had concluded and all countries except the U.S. had signed the treaty at Versailles. The U.S. never did sign it. Four major empires collapsed because of the war: the German, Ottoman, Russian and Hapsburg. The year also marked other historic events: the pandemic Spanish flu of 1918 was still raging; in the U.S., Babe Ruth hit his first home run and then was sold to the Yankees. Also in baseball, the "Black Sox" threw the World Series. Daylight savings time was initiated. Prohibition became the law of the land. The League of Nations was founded. Women's suffrage was gaining inevitable momentum and became law the following year. It was a momentous time in the world.

It was also a critical year for Sam Morse. On the personal side, his mother, Clara, died after a long illness, at his brother Harry's home in San Jacinto, near Los Angeles, and Sam had just married Relda. On the business side, he had just bought a huge piece of property he needed to make profitable. The hotel had recovered but the effects of prohibition, the "noble experiment," were yet to be felt.

The advent of Prohibition in January 1920 put a cloud on the outlook for hotel and restaurant businesses. Then, as now, liquor was a highly profitable part of running these establishments and without booze profit might be elusive. As with many similar operations, the hotel figured a way around the loosely enforced law. Sam even got a head start on the problem.

Sam saw Prohibition on its way. California approved it in January of 1919 and other states were sure to follow. But he had an idea: he contracted to buy five 50-gallon barrels of green whiskey while it was still legal and put them in the basement of one the buildings on the grounds of the hotel. He opened them seven years later in 1926 and tested the booze. Almost 20 percent of the liquid had evaporated and the whiskey was 130 proof, a little strong for bourbon. He found an old "whiskey man" who added distilled water and sherry to bring the bourbon below 100 proof. It was excellent whiskey, and Sam later said he was never as popular as he was then. He remembered giving noted political figure Elihu Root some of the bourbon and the elder statesman was very gratified and said he couldn't sleep without a little sip at bedtime.

Prohibition had specific effects on some people. Sam's friend, Kingsley Macomber had bought 80 acres in Pebble Beach near W. H. Crocker's house. He designed and began construction on a home. The building was unique in Pebble Beach, not Spanish Revival but a log cabin, on steroids. The huge structure featured a ballroom complete with an orchestra balcony, a secret bar, and a fireplace so large you could stand inside it. He never moved in, though. When Prohibition actually became the law, Macomber became upset. He and his wife, Myrtle Harkness, a Standard Oil heiress, moved to Paris, vowing not to return until this idiotic law was repealed. They lived in Paris for the rest of their lives and became major forces in French society, spending their money freely on civic projects and parties. Their major accomplishments included the construction of monuments for French heroes of the American Revolution including General Jean-Baptiste Donatie de Vimeur Rochambeau and Admiral Francois Paul de Grasse. These monuments are at Place Rochambeau and Trocadero Palace.

Their mansion in Pebble Beach stood empty and they asked Sam to have his security check on it. Head of security at the time was Jack Buttle, a tough retired policeman. He knew where to get the alcohol but needed a place to store it. The Macomber place was perfect. Bellhops were told to get their liquor from Jack and nowhere else. Sam did not want anyone at his hotel dying from bathtub gin.

When Macomber bought the land he made a deal with Sam to not subdivide it as long as the Macomber house stood. The company took over the property, probably during the Depression, but the deed restriction limited their ability to develop it. Once again providence provided a solution. Mysteriously, the house burned down in the 1980s and the property was divided up into 15 five-acre home sites. My mother's house, which her daughter Polly designed and her nephew S.F.B. Morse III built, is on one of these lots,

Sam really hated Prohibition even though it was poorly enforced in California. He once said he had rarely seen a woman drunk in public until Prohibition became the law of the land. When it went into effect, guests no longer dined leisurely and danced or strolled about visiting. Instead, they gathered in their rooms for cocktails. Afterwards they staggered downstairs, not having had any food or exercise to even out the effects of alcohol.

Sam told the story of standing on the street in New York City after concluding a deal when he turned to his friend and said, "Lets have a drink to celebrate." His friend said he didn't know of a speakeasy around there. Sam didn't either. They spotted a policeman nearby and Sam suggested they ask him. He went over to the policeman, a big Irish fellow, who gave them a broad grin and pointed to a nearby street saying, "Go down to number 97 and ring three times." They thanked him and enjoyed their celebratory cocktail.

In 1933, when national Prohibition was repealed, each state made up its own rules. Sam was a part of the repeal delegation and the committee putting forth the new rules. He organized other hotel and restaurant owners to propose state laws allowing only hotels and restaurants to serve liquor. The idea was that no booze would be served without food. The law was enacted but bars opened that did not really serve food, with boiled eggs and old sandwiches around to skirt the law.

Despite Prohibition, or possibly because of it, the 1920s were indeed roaring.

Canary Cottage

The Canary (its paint color) Cottage was an interesting annex to the Lodge. The cottage was quite large and served hotel guests as a gambling joint, complete with hookers and booze. The tone was very upscale. Guests wore evening dress and had to be invited. There were roulette and other games and slot machines. Sam was the ultimate hotel man, providing what his guests wanted.

The Cottage was busted twice in November of 1923 and eight months later in July of 1924. There was another official raid before the war for gambling, but this time all the top brass Navy from the flight school were there. The local constabulary gave them a warning.

The Cottage finally closed down as a casino in the 1950s. A slot machine from Canary Cottage was installed in our house. It was very exciting to have the machine in our home. I immediately went to work to figure how to get the quarters out with a screwdriver.

As I write this, the Pebble Beach Company has torn down the former gambling joint and is building additional rooms on the site.

Chapter Thirteen

The Roaring Twenties

At the end of 1919, the new golf course was completed and the construction of the San Clemente dam coming to a close. The Hotel Del Monte resumed its position as a major destination resort and the rich and famous were arriving by the Del Monte Express. Life was good for Sam Morse.

Life got better after the deal closed in 1919. He upgraded the hotel and went into high gear. He hired photographers and publicists to document the beautiful people who came to Monterey. The club theme Sam instituted attracted the young, outdoorsy and athletic types. He had the photogenic ones featured in the socially inclined magazine *Game and Gossip*. Public relations were handled by Herb Cerwin, a brilliant and creative man with the company until WWII.

Sam visited other luxury resorts to see how they attracted guests. It must have been pleasant research. The manager of the famous Poinciana Hotel in Palm Beach gave him a private tour and spelled out his philosophy. Sam saw a piece of the beach roped off and asked why. The manager said it was reserved for the Vanderbilts and Astors and such. The lure of these famous names drew in the hoi polloi.

Sam's philosophy was a little different, but he listened. He would always court the rich and famous, but the artist in him wanted to include everyone to complete his painting. The concept of "hotel as a club" had to have a variety of people. And operating as a club, guests would have full access to all the facilities, an excellent way to attract guests. Everyone wanted to be in the same club with Errol Flynn, Jean Harlow, Charlie Chaplin, Teddy Roosevelt, as well as the Crockers and Vanderbilts. But, he did not want hotel detectives prowling around ruining people's fun.

The '20s introduced the first great building boom on the Peninsula. There was a lot of land to develop and not just for the big houses of Pebble Beach. The future Country Club area held great promise as did the properties Sam controlled in Carmel and Pacific Grove. Pebble Beach was his showcase. Decorators like Francis Adler Elkins were in great demand as were architects Lewis Hobart, Clarence Tantau and George Washington Smith.

Many of the great iconic houses in the area were built in the '20s, and each design had to be personally approved by Sam Morse. He pretty much insisted on the Spanish

Revival style although he made exceptions. Helene Irvin's "Marble Palace" near the Ghost Tree was one. Helene was Templeton Crocker's ex-wife and a Hawaiian sugar heiress. She built a copy of a Travertine Monastery complete with stone towers, a pool filled with sea water and an interior boasting gold faucets in marble bathtubs, hence the name. The interior cost an estimated $2,000,000. Next door to the Marble Palace, Bill Crocker, son of W.H., built a beautiful Spanish style house and next to that, Charles Crocker II commissioned G.W. Smith to build "Videa Vista," where his son now lives. On the hill looking down on these mansions, Cortland Hill, son of the founder of the Great Northern Nekoosa Railroad, built a house his son Jim now owns. Jim says it was the fifth house built

Charcoal drawing by Sam
(See photo on page 104)

in Pebble Beach. The building boom, the new lodge and golf courses and the construction of the clubs in the '20s must have been exciting to witness.

The 1920s were happy for Sam Morse. He had a new wife and a new daughter, Mary, born in September of 1920. He ran a large company developing land as he saw fit and was making money. He drew some very nice cypress trees using charcoal and enjoyed this avocation of drawing and painting for the rest of his life.

He traveled frequently and in luxury. In 1921, he toured Mexico and was hosted by Alvaro Obregon, the president. He loved going to Europe, especially Paris, but

then again, who doesn't? He took long horseback rides in California, learned how to play golf (badly) and enjoyed carousing with his artist friends from Carmel.

After the San Clemente Dam was completed in 1920, he was anxious to sell the rest of his Carmel Valley property. The company replaced the old redwood box pipeline with clay pipes to carry the water to Forest Lake Reservoir in Pebble Beach. From there it was distributed to the cities of Carmel, Monterey and Pacific Grove. Now that the infrastructure was in place, he saw no use for the rest of the land. "There are millions of acres like this in California," he said, when I asked him why he sold it. He would never admit it, but he must have regretted that decision given the value of the property later in his life. He did buy the Holt Ranch in the '60s, now a development with a golf course called Carmel Valley Ranch.

The Blaze, 1924

His string of good luck and good times took a break in 1924 when a fire burned the hotel. The old wooden Victorian structure went up in flames quickly. It must have been quite a sight. Fortunately, a quick-thinking fire captain from the Presidio ordered the main building dynamited before the fire spread. This action saved the two wings with guest rooms. The cause of the fire was uncertain, but Sam suspected it was the giant fireplace in the central entry hall. I know Sam did not like the old fashioned Victorian style but I am also certain this was not one of the "convenient" conflagrations that happened elsewhere on the Monterey Peninsula during this era.

Sam told this story of the night of the fire: he was at his new home, the "President's House," in Pebble Beach. The home was adjacent to the Lodge, perfect for entertaining guests, perched on the 18th fairway with a commanding view of the Pacific and Carmel Bay. When the call came, he rushed over to the hotel but there was little he could do. The place was ablaze. Without really thinking about it, he dashed into the burning building to the drugstore/gift shop. He raced over to the perfume area and grabbed the fanciest bottle and put it in his pocket to give to Relda as a memento, the only surviving bottle from the fire.

He returned home exhausted and collapsed fully dressed on his bed. When he woke up he felt a lump in his pocket and remembered the perfume. He pulled out the bottle and looked at the label for the first time. A bottle of Odorno, a deodorant.

The loss of the main building of the hotel was tough on Sam, but it did not slow him down. He had some insurance and was able to raise money with a bond issue which paid for the rebuilding and allowed him to expand. In the meanwhile, the company erected a tent between the wings to serve as a dining room for the remaining guests. The cottages at the Lodge handled guests for two years while the hotel was building rebuilt.

The New Hotel

Sam was excited to change the look to a more appropriate and attractive design. He wanted the new hotel to reflect Monterey's romantic history and the Spanish influence. The architect, Clarence Tantau, and decorator, Francis Adler Elkins, took the Spanish Revival theme to create a large elegant complex with tile roofs and floors, carved wooden beams and Moorish archways. Sam's artist friends Frank McComas, Paul Whitman and Armen Hanson painted murals depicting the local scenes, history and fantasy.

Tantau added humor in his building plans submitted to the county for permits. Prohibition prompted him to label the Taproom Bar and Grill the "Children's Playroom." No need to tip off the planning department as to the room's real intention. The stuffy Victorian era was gone, and the new young sporting set was arriving.

Hanson and Whitman did a series of paintings for the "Children's Playroom," one depicting a pig with wings upon which sat a naked woman and a clown. This painting was later copied and used as the invitation in the first Bal Masque of the Carmel Art Association. The painting now resides in the Monterey Museum of Art.

The Duke of Alba

Frank McComas painted two murals in the grand entry hall, the first a very large landscape in his soft pastel colors featuring cypress trees at the edge of the Pacific. On the opposite wall, Portolá and Serra land in Monterey in 1778, Serra carries a cross and Portolá a sword. The coat of arms of the Duke of Alba, Count of Monterey, was painted on the downstairs dining hall, and Sam invited the current duke to come visit. His ancestor was governor of Mexico at the time Monterey was discovered by the Spanish. The duke did come in 1926 as part of a California tour and they planted a redwood tree near the front entrance of the hotel to commemorate the visit. It stands today bearing a plaque with their names. *(See photo on page 55)*

McComas took some liberty with the Peninsula mural. He had recently been arrested in Pacific Grove for drunk driving and, in his opinion, was treated badly. In revenge he wiped Pacific Grove off his map and renamed the town Moss Beach.

Father Mestres and the Carmel Mission

When the current Duke of Alba, Count of Monterey, stayed at the Hotel Del Monte, he expressed an interest in visiting the Old Carmel Mission, San Carlos Borroméo de Carmelo. The mission fell into disrepair in the 1830s after the Spanish left and the missions and lands were secularized. Later in that century the buildings were given back to the church and a new pastor built a roof, saving it from collapse and further deterioration.

In 1919 the pastor of the Mission, Father Ramon Mestres started restoring the church and hired famed sculptor Jo Mora to oversee the project to make it as authentic as possible. This had been the headquarters of the 21 missions Junípero Serra established in California. Despite negative judgments of Serra from a 21st century perspective, he did teach the local Indians agriculture as well as the catechism. He was stern with them in the same way parents were with their children, but he did not enslave them or whip them as is often fantasized.

Sam took the current duke on a tour of the Peninsula ending at the mission where they were greeted by Father Mestres. As they toured, Sam noticed an odd cross laid on Serra's grave that looked handmade from a tree. When asked about it, Father Mestres said:

"It is an interesting story, that cross, and how it came to be here. When I first arrived in Carmel, I was approached by an Indian man. He asked me to come out to the Cachagua to see his dying elderly grandmother who had asked for me. She was ill and could not travel.

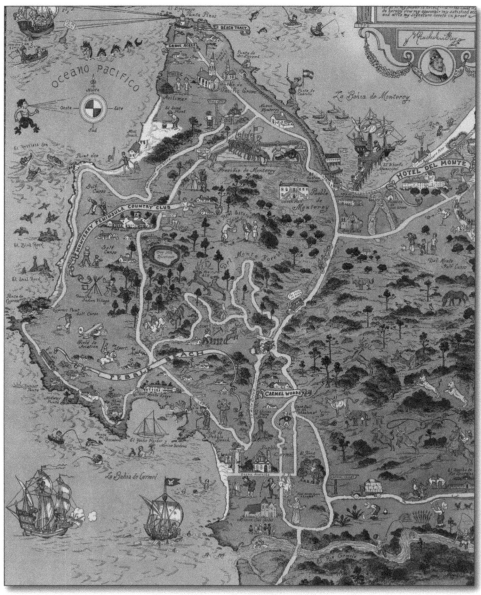

Detail of map by Jo Mora, 1926
(See full map on page xiii)

"The Cachagua is a rough, barely accessible, mountainous piece of land about 30 miles up the Carmel Valley. Many Indians moved there, as the rules and habits of Anglo Carmel had driven them out. I agreed to go see the dying woman and packed a blanket and rations on my mule and set out on the journey. I arrived later that night and went to see the old woman. She lived in a one-room shack and was in bed when I arrived. After speaking with her I settled down on the floor near her bed to spend the night. I noticed a strange looking cross up in the rafters, and asked her about it.

"The old Indian woman told me her grandfather, a Mission Indian, had taken it from the mission when it was secularized (1834) as he was afraid it would fall into the wrong hands.

"The cross was very special. Apparently when Serra was traveling to Monterey he noticed a Manzanita tree growing in the shape of a cross. He had his soldiers cut it down and carried it with him to Carmel. He installed the cross in the mission court-yard where it stood for years. At his death, it was placed on his grave. When the missions were closed in 1830 her grandfather went to Carmel, took the cross and brought it home with him. It sat where it was now for 75 years. She wanted me to take it back to the mission where it belonged."

So this odd looking tree/cross was hand-picked personally by Father (now Saint) Junípero Serra as an important piece of the mission. The Duke of Alba, Count of Monterey was impressed with the restoration work as well as the story. The tree/cross is still in the Mission museum.

While at the Carmel Mission, the Duke met Jo Mora who presented him with an historical map of Monterey featuring the Duke's coat of arms. Mora was working on the sarcophagus of Serra and the duke was impressed with Mora's art. The artist of Spanish descent from Uruguay must have been proud.

Carmel, Devendorf and Powers

Jo Mora lived in Carmel at the time, but Sam offered him a lot in Pebble Beach. Frank Devendorf, one of the two founders of Carmel had given Jo a lot in Carmel and perhaps was not very happy that Sam lured him away.

Carmel was incorporated in 1916, but Frank Devendorf and Frank Powers started a bohemian community there earlier. Artists, writers and performers comprised 65 percent of the town's population, imbuing it with the unique character still evident today. Sam had many artist friends who lived in Carmel and he enjoyed their activities. He may not have agreed with their progressive politics, but they were fun-loving, free spirits which Sam liked: campfires on the beach, impromptu plays in the forest and constant cocktail parties. He joined in the bonfires and knew all the verses of the Abalone Song. In his memoirs, written when he was over 80, he dictated some of the verses to his secretary, Margaret.

The Abalone Song goes somewhat as follows:

The Abalone Song

There are some folks like quail on toast
Because they think it's tony,
But I'm content to owe my rent
And live on abalone.

He wanders free beneath the sea
Where e'er the coast is stony
He flaps his wings and gayly sings
The festive abalone.

The more we take the more they make
In deep sea matrimony,
Race suicide does not betide
the fertile abalone.

Some drink wine and some champagne
Or brandy by the pony
But I will try a little rye
With a dash of abalone.

Some like lamb and some like ham
And some like macaroni,
But bring me in a pail of gin
And a tub of abalone.

I'll telegraph my better half
By Morse or by Marconi;
But when I need a lot of speed,
I'll send an abalone.

And so forth, until the final verse:

Some think that the Lord is fat
And some think He is bony;
But as for me I think that He
Is like an abalone.

Chapter Fourteen

River Ranch

In 1925, while Devendorf and Powers developed the Carmel Highlands and built an inn, Sam was busy offloading land, including most of Carmel Valley. He offered it at $150 an acre in 1921 with no takers. Finally, he dropped the price to $125 and divided the acreage into 11 parcels. Marion Hollins, Helen Crocker Russell (daughter of W. H. Crocker), William Porter of Salinas and a local real estate group including his brother-in-law, Byington Ford, snapped up some of the parcels.

In 1926, Relda insisted he buy some of the Carmel Valley property back. She was tired of the foggy summers in Pebble Beach and wanted her own place in the valley. Although he had sold some of the eleven parcels, one choice site was available. Sam knew the area well and, as fog avoidance was the goal, he carefully selected 500 acres past the coastal fog line, not too far from Pebble Beach and sufficient to meet Relda's request. He called the place River Ranch.

Three miles downstream from the River Ranch, Robinson Canyon meets Carmel Valley. The river takes a sharp turn and the geology is such that it creates a barrier to the coastal marine layer. If you are at River Ranch you can see the edge of the fog blanket over the valley to the west. We call the distant fog "Boss's Wall."

The Ranch sits below Garzas Creek on the Carmel River and even in dry years the river always runs right there. Downstream it disappears underground for most of its journey to the sea as the Cal Am pumping stations siphon off most of the water. Willows and sycamores grow along the banks while live oaks pepper the landscape higher up.

The river separates the ranch houses, bunkhouses, corrals, barns, chicken coops, warehouse and the stables from the fields and riding trails on the other side. Sam's suspension bridge over the river lasted 57 years, surviving major floods until an El Niño in 1983 washed it away. One tower collapsed and we had to cut the cables suspending the bridge during the height of the flood. A young cowboy lassoed our bridge at the Farm Center bridge and offered to sell it to us. We declined.

In the summer when the river was at a low level, Sam's road crews came out from Pebble Beach and created a temporary boulder dam. The lake created went upstream almost half a mile, providing us with an excellent fishing and crawdad hunting environment. When winter returned the temporary dam was washed away by the high water, and migrating fish found their spawning grounds.

Sam selected a home-site near but slightly above the river with a fine view of a big meadow and the ridges to the west. The building began with a brick barbecue, built initially for picnics during the house construction and has been in continuous use ever since. I like to say Sam built the first house, what we call the River House, on a Sunday afternoon in 1926. The construction was a quick and easy process. The floor, which also operates as the foundation, is highly polished red brick; the single walls board-and-batten built on the ground then tilted up and fastened together with no internal wall, thus no insulation. The living room is Palladian in proportion and has a large centrally positioned fireplace, which comes complete with an inglenook, an

iron arm for holding a pot, and an oven space in the bricks on the side with an iron door. The mantel is a ten foot piece of roughly milled redwood. On the mantel he hung his father's Enfield musket from the Civil War. It hang there today. The fireplace heats the large room quickly, assisted by the relatively low ceiling of exposed beams. My sister Polly, the architect, designed subtle skylights in 1998 providing much needed light in the daytime.

In Sam's time the walls were covered in antique weapons, including a blunderbuss and a 4 gauge shotgun used for elephant hunting, swords and daggers, spears and clubs. A giant paddle-shaped tiller leaned in one corner next to what we were told were slave chains. At his death, the family gave these treasures to the Presidio in Monterey, now on in display in the army base library. I note that Sam was not a hunter and had an aversion to killing animals unnecessarily, but he did enjoy the artistry of well-crafted pieces.

The dining room is perfectly proportioned to seat 6 to 14 people around a hand-made table with matching spindle chairs, buffet and cupboard. All the original furniture is still in place. We remodeled the kitchen a few years ago, on the same footprint. On the other side of the barbecue, upstream from the living room complex sits the three-bedroom three-bath sleeping quarters. It is connected to the River House by a trellis with an ancient wisteria vine.

The River Ranch dining room

Over the years, Sam built additional housing: first servants' quarters, bunkhouse and foreman's house, then a playhouse for his daughter, Mary and eventually a separate house for himself and his third wife, Maurine. A large hay barn had stalls for several horses and a warehouse full of treasures including WWII memorabilia, old photographs and odd furniture, where I spent many hours of discovery. He added a large oval shaped pool and pool houses further down the river and a sandbox filled with the fine white sand of Pebble Beach.

Sam took special guests out to Carmel Valley to the River Ranch in summer to escape the fog and sometimes just for privacy. Carmel Valley is only a 20-minute car ride from Pebble Beach but the weather is dramatically different; instead of the foggy overcast lasting most of the day, the valley is clear in the summer by 10am and stays that way until late evening.

He had horses and a pleasant place to ride. On the other side of the river was a large open field to gallop along and then back to the stream to water your horse. The trails wound through the hills to the top of the ridge and the border to George Gordon Moore's Rancho San Carlos.

Sam sat well in the saddle -- with many years of riding in the Central Valley, he certainly knew how. His favorite horse was Moonlight. He said he "loved that horse from the time he was a colt until I shot him," (when Moonlight was old and infirm and shooting the preferred cowboy method of euthanizing their ponies.)

There were many wealthy and self indulgent characters in the '20s and '30s. One was George Gordon Moore, whose ranch has been subdivided extensively and is now known as The Preserve. In Moore's day, when the ranch was his private game preserve, he imported exotic animals like 500 pound Russian boars. These animals still roam the Coastal Range but are becoming rare. There is record at the River Ranch of one killed by a ranch hand.

Tony Vasquez, grand-nephew of the famous bandit Tiburcio Vasquez, excellent at breaking horses, was one of Sam's favorite hands at the River Ranch. Tony and the other hands had a bunkhouse and kitchen away from the main house. The foreman had separate quarters and a small guesthouse stood next door.

Never a real working ranch but a rich man's summer place, it did boast a large Shetland pony herd in the 1950s. Shetlands were thought to be a good way to introduce youngsters to the joy of riding at horse ranches, circuses, fairs and stables around the country, but they were ungainly little beasts with stubborn attitudes and concrete mouths. Captain Topper, the stud at River Ranch, was different: a handsome palomino with more horse-like proportions than the standard barrel-chested Shetland. The Shetland pony craze in the U.S. died quickly in the late 1950s when people got tired of being bitten while sitting atop an unresponsive nag. The herd was sold off and replaced by cattle to graze on the land across the river.

Stars

The ranch was a place to bring special guests of the hotel and later the Lodge. Some favorites included Gov. Earl Warren, Lana Turner, William Powell and Jean Harlow. (Powell and Harlow spent most of their time in the bedroom, per a precocious Miss Mary Morse.) Sir Anthony Eden retreated there and did work on his speech on forming the United Nations in 1945.

While at the ranch, Jean Harlow taught 15-year-old Mary Morse how to milk a cow. The movie star grew up on a farm and loved animals. In the picture below she was 25 years old and at the height of her career. Harlow died the next year in 1936 from a blood disease.

River Ranch boasts a mural over the bar by Frank McComas and several paintings by Frank's wife, Gene Francis. Frank's real name was Francis and Gene often went by her

Jean Harlow and William Powell

married name, so we often confused the two: Gene Francis McComas and Francis McComas. A large framed charcoal by Gene depicting a Mexican plaza sits outside on the brick patio under an awning. It has been there for over 80 years and appears to be in perfect shape.

The Haida House

One house at the ranch with an interesting history was built in San Francisco and then brought down to the property on a truck. In 1941, the World's Fair on Treasure Island in San Francisco was drawing to a close. In the Western States exhibit, which included both U.S. and Canada, a young man named Dudley Carter built an authentic Haida Indian lodge. With his axe, knives, and froes, he carved and shaped and built the lodge using ancient techniques. There are pictures of Carter carving and chopping in booklets about the fair. No nails, screws or steel are in the construction; everything cut then cleverly fitted together. The front door was built into a 15-foot Haida Totem pole with raven and bear totems. The lower section of the pole a door set on sturdy carved wooden hinges which opened inward. The closing device was a carved wooden frog mounted next to the door inside which swung down into the locking position. A raised plat-form attached to one side of the house served as a sleeping area—very cozy and private and where I'm sure half my relatives lost their virginity.

When the war broke out in 1941 and the fair closed, Carter disassembled the lodge, loaded it onto a flatbed truck and drove down the coast to Carmel. He received permission from Flip Hatton to set up the lodge at the mouth of the Carmel River. Sam heard about it and went to see it. He was very impressed and Carter agreed to sell it to him for $500. Sam moved it out to the ranch, located it facing the swimming pool and commissioned Carter to build a second little house next to it.

We had to take the "Haida House" down in 1978. The fireplace had been built over an abandoned septic tank which was pulling the house apart. The family decided to move the whole thing down to a piece of family property in the South Coast section of Big Sur. We found Dudley Carter in Vancouver, British

Sam with Ginger Rogers
at the River Ranch 1940

Columbia, then in his late 80s and in good health. He came down and supervised the move and the reconstruction of the house, did additional carving, made all the shingles by hand, and set the house on redwood rounds. It's now in the middle of an ecological preserve on a rise above a large clear running creek, about a mile inland from the sea. Although the house is made of cedar, it fits well into the large redwood grove. As a 100th birthday present to Dudley Carter, his daughter, granddaughter and great-granddaughter came to Big Sur and posed in front of the house. This "Haida House" was his favorite of all his work in museums in San Francisco, Vancouver B.C., etc. The little house he built in the Haida fashion remains at the ranch next to the pool. We converted it from a changing room to a very pleasant guest room by adding a bathroom with an outdoor shower and two tubs.

In the '30s and '40s the Del Monte Lodge set up publicity photos at River Ranch with celebrities and Sam *playing* cowboy: playing because he was over 50 years old and had been recently riding desks more than horses.

Sam loved the ranch. It reminded him of his youthful work in the Central Valley. He carried on the big rough-rider role all his life and often told stories about those times. The ranch was also a great place to relax, entertain and have parties. We estimate that there have been almost a thousand parties there since 1926. It was also the only home Sam kept throughout his life. His first home in Pebble Beach was part of the Lodge and was demolished to make more guest rooms. His widow, Maurine, willed their final home to the Community Hospital of the Monterey Peninsula (CHOMP).

In Sam's will he instructed his executor, Justin Dart, to scatter his ashes over River Ranch. Justin's wife, Jane Rexall Dart, told me years later at a dinner party that some of the ashes made it, most flew back into the plane. One of Sam's sons, John Boit (Jack) Morse, had his own ashes scattered there, not from an airplane but by the hands of his son, Rickie and grandson, Bredon.

The grazing areas and farm portion of River Ranch were sold at Sam's death to raise money for estate taxes. The buyer, Jim Garland, owned it for two or three years, never lived there, and then sold it to the county for a slight discount if they named it after him. It is now an undeveloped public recreational area. The ranch house and guest houses remain in the family and we continue to enjoy them.

Chapter Fifteen

Family Life, 1920s Pebble Beach

The year 1920 introduced Mary Morse to the world in September and she was the apple of Sam's eye. Although he was not one for expressing emotions, he loved spending time with his little girl and showered her with affection.

Mary enjoyed encounters with movie stars and sports figures. Her golf guru, Marion Hollins, was the women's amateur champion in 1921. As mentioned, Jean Harlow taught Mary how to milk a cow. Errol Flynn gave Mary her first gin and tonic, leaned back and said, "I do believe I've kissed a virgin." He then tried to seduce the 15 year old. She said recently that she often second guessed herself about her refusal of his advances: give it up to Errol Flynn or wait for her marriage day? One deterrent was that Sam would beat Flynn senseless if he found out. One day, Olympic swimmer and Tarzan, Johnny Weissmuller escorted her around Pebble Beach with her girlfriend. Tarzan sat in the middle and put his big muscular arms around the two of them. She said it was very cozy. Salvador Dali insisted she sit next to him at dinner parties. She spoke French and he pretended not to speak English. It didn't hurt that she was attractive as well.

Sam and Mary at the Pebble Beach Equestrian Center, circa 1927

Joan Fontaine was a regular tennis partner of Mary's. Later in life she told Mary she almost became her stepmother. I asked Ms. Fontaine about that just before she passed away in 2014. She said it was in 1952. Sam had lost Relda in 1951 and Fontaine was between husbands. He took her out to the ranch to show off his new dam and lake. Although the romance was hot and heavy, she told me they decided it would not work out. She was not ready to leave Hollywood, and he would not leave Pebble Beach.

Mary learned how to play golf from Cam Puget and Peter Hay, two of the best teaching pros in the West. Her governess, Mademoiselle DuMont, had her hit 100 golf balls a day while Mademoiselle knitted. Their practice tee was the 18th at Pebble Beach, in front of her parents' house. Mademoiselle also taught Mary French. Mary went on to become an accomplished golfer and had the course records at Pebble Beach, Cypress Point Club, San Francisco Golf Club and Stanford. She was a semi-finalist in the Women's Championship in 1938, losing to the eventual winner, Patty Berg.

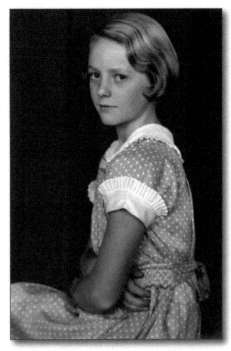

Photo of Mary by Edward Weston

Mary gave up golf in her early 20s; it was more a burden than a pleasure, with two exceptions. In 1958 she followed her father at Cypress Point on the day he played with President Eisenhower. Her playing partner was her friend Bud Allen, owner of the La Playa Inn.

The other exception was on a bet with the former Stanford and 49ers quarterback, Frankie Albert. In the early sixties they were at a party at her father's house, the "President's House" next to the Lodge. Mary was about 45. The party was going strong in the late sunlight of summer when a good friend of Mary's, Mackie Leonard, set up the bet. She teased Albert that a woman could probably beat him at golf. He, a big tough football player and an excellent athlete, said no woman could beat him. The crowd got Mary to agree to play the 18th hole. Albert went home, got his clubs, put on his spikes, and went down to the tee. The par-five 18th hole, redesigned by Sam, hugs the ocean for the entire 543 yards, is well trapped and has trees in the most awkward places. Jack Nicklaus called it the best finishing hole in golf.

Mary, being the female, went first. She took off her heels to play barefoot and borrowed a five-iron from someone. This must have bothered Frankie. She drove a reasonable ball down the middle. Albert put his first two shots in the ocean. He never recovered. Mary ended up with a double bogey seven using the five-iron the whole way, including turning it around and putting left handed. Mackie won the bet and Albert never got over the humiliation of losing to a woman. He and Mary were at Stanford at about the same time, and he surely knew of her reputation. No doubt alcohol fueled his hubris.

A few years later I saw him at a party. I knew his daughter, Janie, from tennis but barely knew him. He perhaps still stung from the golf fiasco; with little provocation he put me in a headlock and told me I needed a haircut. He was laughing, but I was not.

Mary's mother, Relda, was loving but distant. The pressure of being married to Sam, constantly entertaining and traveling, wore her down. She turned to the bottle for friendship. Sam and Mary tried to steer her away from alcohol, but were not successful. Relda died in 1951 from heart failure when I was just 4 years old. I have only a few memories of her as an elegant and friendly but aloof woman.

Being forced to play golf and raised in "splendid isolation," may not sound too bad to a lot of people, but it basically stole her childhood. As soon as she graduated from Stanford in 1942, she moved to New York and sold advertisements for a magazine.

She married Richard Osborne in 1943 at the River Club in New York. He was on leave from the Navy and went back to the Pacific Theater after the wedding. She returned to California. In September of 1944, she gave birth to her first child, Susan Morse Osborne, in the old Carmel Hospital. Susan now lives at the River Ranch in the expanded and remodeled playhouse built for her mother.

Sam was on good terms with his former wife, Anne's, new husband, George Richardson, and communicated with him regarding expenses for the children and their education. He rarely wrote to Anne. Judging from the letters saved at the Stanford Library, Sam was very judgmental about his children: if they did not write regularly or had poor grades at school, he scolded them. If they complained, he ignored the complaint and told them in essence to *suck it up.*

Sam Jr., Jack and Nancy

Sam's three children from his marriage to Anne were raised in Lake Forest, Illinois. They would come out to River Ranch in the summers. As they grew older they spent more time in California and all of them lived in or near Pebble Beach at some point in their lives. Nancy, the youngest, was incredibly charming and funny. Jack, the middle child, started in business and ended as an artist. He was a recovering alcoholic with his father's strong views on everything. He told me once that if you want to be a writer then write every day, even if it is your laundry list. I did not know Sam Jr. or Sammy, as his life ended when I was 2 years old. My mother says he was the nicest of them all.

Sammy may have had PTSD from the war, but that diagnosis didn't exist then. A few years after the war he "made the mistake of taking too many sleeping pills," the

Sam and his four children. Left to right: Jack, Nancy, Sam, Mary, Sam Jr.

family explanation for his death. He was a poor student and could not stick to much of anything. He was very well liked by all but lived in the shadow of his father, had an unhappy marriage, and ended his life at an early age.

Sam Jr.'s only child, Sam III, or Sammy3 to the family, turned to S.F.B. for paternal guidance, but old Sam was never one for this task. He could be quite brusque with his family and Sammy3 got a little wild. During college, he dated the daughter of a famous movie star. One night he borrowed his girlfriend's sports car without bothering to tell her. The car was registered in her mother's name. The girlfriend reported it stolen and he got arrested. Headlines the next day said, "S.F.B. Morse steals Ingrid Bergman's car." He was humiliated, of course. The final blow came about two weeks later when a clipping service sent S.F.B. a notice saying, "Your name has appeared in the New York Times. If you would like a copy please send us $5 and a return envelope." He didn't.

Sammy3 now lives in Santa Fe, is happily married to Joan and has two successful and beautiful grown daughters.

Sam Sr.'s second son, Jack, and I once talked about his alcoholism. He started life as a golden boy, in S.F.B.'s mold: barrel-chested, an athlete at Yale, worked for his father at Del Monte, a mistake. Jack had three strong father figures in his life and needed to be out on his own, away from their influence.

His step-father, George Richardson, was a force in Chicago, the trustee of the Marshall Field estate, an all-encompassing affair as the estate not only controlled the giant department store of the same name but multiple other enterprises. He was a fair-minded man, but strong-willed like Sam.

Jack's "third father" was another Chicagoan. Jack married the daughter of Donald McClennan, senior executive of Marsh & McClennan insurance company, the largest in the U. S. Needless to say, McClennan also had a strong personal presence.

It was under the gaze of these three uncompromising, successful men that Jack grew into adulthood. He, like Relda, turned to drink as an antidote to the pressures of life.

It wasn't until the early '60s after his father publicly fired him from Del Monte and his first wife, Margaret, left him that Jack stopped drinking and began painting full time. He married a fellow recovering alcoholic and artist, Virginia Bailhe. They lived a full life traveling and fixing up houses. Their bohemian lifestyle suited them both and they were a pleasure to be around. Jack and his first wife, Margaret, had two children, Peter and Richardson (Rickie) Morse. Peter, an avid collector and expert on Japanese prints, especially Hokusai, passed away in 1995. Rickie lives on a ranch in Southern California after a Hollywood career as an actor and producer.

Nancy was the youngest of the three and she was a lively, fun figure whom we all adored. Seven years older than Mary, she spent most of her early life in Chicago. After college, she moved to California and married her first husband, Lent Hooker. They had two children, Michael and Rodman. Michael lives in San Francisco and is a stock broker like his father. He and I are good friends, and we see each other often. His brother, Rod, became a banker in Seattle and passed away in 2016 in Palm Desert.

The marriage to Lent did not last long, and Nancy married Kenneth Walker of Chicago and had one child, Elizabeth, known as Jabby. Her third husband, William Borland, was another Chicagoan and also a stockbroker. Nancy's daughter Jabby lives in Connecticut, but I have not seen her since the day Walt Disney surprised us at the ranch in 1965.

My Minute with Walt Disney

It was a strange day when Sam brought his friend Walt to the River Ranch. Cousin Jabby was staying in the River House with my parents and sister Susan in residence. Susan and Jabby were about the same age and were friends. I was sleeping in the "Haida House" with my disreputable teenage buddies, five of us camping out or rather passed out after consuming all the cigarettes and beer we could find. It was about 9AM when the door slowly opened. We were all still asleep, but I woke up in time to see Boss and Walt Disney looking in at the horror -- five disheveled teenage boys in a room full of stale beer and tobacco stink. They silently closed the door and left. I hurriedly got up and dressed and went to look for my childhood icon. Sadly, they had retreated to Sam's house, where I dared not tread without an invitation. Jabby and Susan were also out looking for Disney. He did not reappear.

Susan had met him before on opening day of Disneyland in 1955. She arrived at the park by helicopter and got a tour from the great man himself, riding in a golf cart. Apparently, he was a very nice man who loved animals and small children, in that order.

I was not invited to Disneyland.

Chapter Sixteen

Temptress of the South Seas

Sam recommended getting out of the office and enjoying yourself and he did not have a problem with how much time that took. Trips to Europe and South America lasted weeks or months but he made that work and his business did not suffer. Going for a ride or playing golf or visiting friends could eat up a day, but it was all worth it to Sam. Toward the end of the 1920s he traveled a long way to a place he had only daydreamed about, the South Seas.

On a trip to Paris in 1928 he and two friends, Stan Gwin and Gordon Armsby, talked about sailing to the South Seas, in their opinion an adventure every young man should take. On January 2, 1929 at about noon, Sam first saw *The Temptress* docked in San Francisco and fell in love. By 12:10 she was his.

The two-masted schooner was originally built by the Canadian government for coastal geostatic work, "whatever that is," said Sam. John Gilbert, the movie star, had it completely refurbished as a pleasure boat and named her *The Temptress* after a movie starring Greta Garbo. Garbo

The Temptress in Tahiti

was not a keen sailor so Gilbert sold the boat. *The Temptress* was 105 feet long with a 20-foot beam, three comfortable staterooms, crews' quarters, a separate captain's cabin, a complete galley, a large salon and a powerful engine to augment the sail power.

Sam contracted his friend, Bull Lion, to be the skipper and they began planning the trip to the South Seas immediately. A crew was put together, including a mate and a wireless operator named Louis who was terrified for the entire trip and the only one to get seasick. After provisioning the ship, Stan and Gordon sailed down to Pebble Beach to meet Sam.

The distance from Pebble Beach to Tahiti is 4,171 miles and they planned a stop at the Marquesas on the way, three weeks out and the steamer back, perhaps another week. Relda came along, and later they met up with Gene McComas and Templeton Crocker. Just before the trip, Temp's cousin, Bill Crocker, presented them with a parrot. Unfortunately, the only thing the parrot could say was, "Good morning, Mr. Crocker." They left the parrot behind and took along a small dog as the boat pet.

While sailing in the South Seas, Sam ran into his old Yale friend (Charles) Templeton Crocker. Templeton's yacht, *Zaca*, was a beautiful sight and still has some fame: the St. Francis Yacht Club has a full-scale model of it and Templeton named his private camp in Bohemian Grove, Zaca. His nephew Frederick Crocker Whitman took it over after Temp died.

Templeton Crocker (1884-1948)
on *Zaca*, c. 1929

Although he and Sam were friends in college, their paths diverged in their adult lives. Sam was likely still peeved at the Crockers' rejection when he went to them for funding in 1919, but each man had changed with maturity. Sam had toughened up from his cowboy years in the Central Valley and was all business or all fun in everything he did.

When they met up in Tahiti, Temp was devoting his life to oceanography, art, and music. Templeton married the heiress Helene Irwin in a huge society wedding in Burlingame. Her father, a partner with Claus Spreckels in the Hawaiian sugar business, gave her $1,000,000 as a wedding present. Although the gift was appreciated, the marriage wasn't. Helene soon asked Templeton for a divorce. It turns out he preferred a bachelor's life, and the marriage was a sham. In the divorce proceedings, Helene got the Ghost Tree lot.

The pictures from that trip show a very relaxed Sam Morse. He wrote a monograph about it called "The Temptress of the South Seas." Accompanying his drawings were detailed accounts of the people he met and the uniqueness of the islands. Sam wrote in his monograph that Templeton's *Zaca* was moored nearby at one stop, but he does not mention seeing him. Their different lives left them with little to say.

The group took a steamer home from Tahiti and late in the summer of 1929 Sam sold *The Temptress*. Perfect timing, given what happening in the economy.

Yachting Ladies

Chapter Seventeen

The Pebble Beach Clubs, 1920s

In keeping with his view of the hotel as a club and Pebble Beach as the sports area, sporting events, golf and country clubs and sports teams were a big part of Sam's Monterey Peninsula, ranging from the exclusive to the ordinary. He was a founding member of Cypress Point Club in Pebble Beach and the Old Capital Club in Monterey. He was the first baseman for the Shamrocks baseball team of the Abalone League and on the Del Monte polo team. He created the Beach and Tennis Club in Pebble Beach and the Monterey Peninsula Country Club. He loved the outdoors and found sport in it everywhere. He was not a hunter though, especially after that coyote chase in his Central Valley days.

The first big golf tournament in Pebble Beach was the California Amateur in 1919, an annual tournament event at Pebble for another 45 years until the association rotated it to other courses. When the tournament moved to Pebble Beach, it was a major accomplishment. It was the premier golf tournament in the state and quite a feather in Sam's cap to bring it to a brand-new golf course. There were few professional tournaments at the time and amateurs were still winning the majors.

In the excellent book, *The Match*, author Mark Frost describes the transition from amateur domination to professional. In 1956 a pair of amateurs, Ken Venturi and Harvie Ward, teamed up against a pair of professionals, Byron Nelson and Ben Hogan, to play one round at Cypress Point. Befitting the time, the match was set up by two millionaires, a car dealer and the scion of an oil fortune. If the match were held today, the pros would walk all over the amateurs, but in 1956 it was anyone's guess. The book is well written and I will not reveal the winner of the match.

Earlier in the century there was a social stigma about the game: it belonged to the rich and golf pros were hired underlings. Most pros were not allowed to play in tournaments because they were not members of the clubs where the tournaments were held. This changed after the war and a few top golfers started making real money and gaining some fame.

Sam set up Pebble Beach as the sports area of Del Monte. There was golf at Pebble, polo and equestrian events at the stables nearby and multiple tennis courts and a pool at the Beach Club. A small harbor and pier nestled in Stillwater Cove next to the Beach Club, and miles of trails out of the stables for the casual rider. There was also archery, swimming, and gambling. What it lacked was an area of smaller homes and a country club. A conversation with General James Harbord stationed at nearby Fort Ord, planted the

Monterey Peninsula Country Club

seed. The general, General John Pershing's second-in-command, mentioned to Sam that many personnel were quite fond of the area, and would love to retire there. Sam ran with the idea in 1925.

The Monterey Peninsula Country Club (MPCC) was unique in its development. A group of retired military men formed a club while Sam built the clubhouse and golf course and developed the lots. He then sold the lots to the retired military who became members of the club. In other words, first you were deemed acceptable by the other members, then you bought a lot and were officially admitted into the club. The lots were set back in the forest, away from the course, to enhance the beauty of the links. Lots uniformly sold for $1,500. At first the lots sold quickly, and the membership flourished, but when the Depression hit, sales slowed to nothing. Club dues were $2.50 a month with no initiation fee if you bought a lot.

In the late 1940's and early 1950's my father Richard Osborne was the club manager. The company wanted to turn the course over to the members, but the members didn't want the expense of maintenance. They enjoyed their low dues while taking full advantage of the amenities.

In order to convince them it was a very good deal, Sam promised to build them a second course known as the Shore Course as a sweetener. This sealed the deal, and the MPCC continues to this day as a private club. In 2015 they tore up the original Dunes Course and built one far more spectacular in its place. Sam's Shore Course, after some remodeling in 2003, remains.

The next club to be built was dreamed up by Marion Hollins.

Sam showing the layout for the Shore Course of the Country Club

The Cypress Point Club; Marion Hollins

Marion was Sam's top salesperson and a former U.S. Women's Amateur Golf champion. She had boundless energy with a disarmingly sweet personality. She was a dreamer with big ideas which got her into trouble on and off all her life.

Marion felt MPCC was a good idea but she thought the company might sell more lots in the pricey Pebble Beach area if there were an exclusive golf club. Pebble Beach was and has always been a public course. She optioned the land she needed from Sam and set out to find members for her soon-to-be Cypress Point Club.

Cypress was designed for the just the "right" people, an exclusive club with limited membership of 100 golfers. The first members were a mix of local and San Francisco society. Others from the East and Southern California were added quickly. The first to join included several Crocker family members, Harry Hunt, and locals Francis McComas, the painter, and Harold Mack, a partner of financier Bernard Baruch. Sam sold the land to the club and took back a note for the purchase.

Marion enlisted Alistair McKenzie as course architect. The course hugs the shoreline with large sand dunes behind it and carves its way through a thick pine forest before emerging on the coast. The clubhouse, designed by architect George Washington Smith, sits atop a knoll amidst cypress trees with a commanding

Marion Hollins (1892-1944)

view of the ocean and the golf course. During construction, they discovered an old Indian burial site. Interestingly, all the remains had their feet pointed out to the sea.

One of Marion's key contributions to Cypress was the location of the pin on the famous 16th hole. As she and McKenzie laid out the course, they came to a small bay with a jutting rocky peninsula. Marion dropped a ball on the ground and hit a three iron over the bay. Pointing to the place the ball landed she said, "Put the pin there." And they did.

The club was an immediate success and reached full membership quickly. People were so awed by the natural beauty and the thrill of it they ignored the toughness of the course.

As with the country club, however, the timing was not good. During the Depression membership fell to 14, and the club looked likely to close. They could not take care of the property with dues at practically nothing. Sam took over maintenance of the course and forgave the debt. He did not want a high-publicity failure attached to Pebble Beach.

The Depression was very unkind to Marion, who had many twists and turns in her very eventful life.

Marion was born in 1892 in East Islip, N. Y, the youngest child of five and the only daughter born to Harry and Evalina Hollins. He was a wealthy stock broker in New York and friend of J.P. Morgan and William Vanderbilt. Marion followed her big brothers around their 250-acre estate on Long Island and became the classic tomboy. She was an excellent equestrian and could compete in any sport, became the most accomplished female polo player in the country and was a regular in men's games. She was also the first woman to compete in a mixed company car race. She started the first women's golf club, the Women's National in Glen Head, N.Y. Golf was her favorite sport and she was good at it. She won the 1921 U.S. Women's Amateur championship, the first of several tournament successes.

When her father lost his money in a bank collapse, Marion set out on her own. In 1922, she moved to California and met Sam. He was

Marion on her polo pony

immediately impressed and offered her the job of athletic director of Pebble Beach. She accepted and became an integral part of his team. Her friendly approach to life, her creative ambition, and her excellent East Coast connections helped him enormously. Cypress Point was her grandest achievement but she had other ventures.

Marion was a dreamer with grand plans. Unfortunately, many were poorly timed. Late in the '20s she had good luck when an inherited oil well struck a gusher. She sold it for $2 million and began her career as a developer.

Marion bought vast acreage in Big Sur to build a golf resort: several ranches from old-time settlers in Big Sur and the Marble family and combined them for a total of 8,000 acres. There was no highway, but one was planned. It was and is a beautiful piece of land -- redwood groves, several running streams, hot springs and three miles of beautiful coastline viewed from the ridges of Big Sur. One of the better-known residents of Big Sur was Lillian Bos Ross. She and her husband, Harry Dick

Ross (his real name), lived on Marion's property. While there Lillian wrote *Zandy's Bride* (later a movie with Gene Hackman) and *The Ballad of the South Coast*, a poem popularized in the 1950s song by the Kingston Trio.

Marion started on the development of the Big Creek Resort prematurely, building roads and bridges with local contractors such as the Harlans and Trotters. William Wooster, a brilliant young local architect, designed and built a cabin next to the hot springs. He went on to acclaim as head of University of California Berkeley's school of architecture.

At the same time in the late '20s, Marion developed Pasatiempo Golf Course in Scotts Valley near Santa Cruz, California. She wanted another Cypress Point. She hired McKenzie to design the course and built herself a grand home. She was beginning to sell lots and the clubhouse when Wall Street crashed in October of 1929.

Marion ran out of money and was forced to abandon both projects, selling the Big Sur property to an eccentric Nabisco heir, Edward S. Moore, who called the ranch the Circle M. Today the property is part of the University of California Natural Preserve System. Her creditors took over all of Pasatiempo, including her home. One night as she drove home, a drunk driver smashed into her, causing lasting physical and mental injuries and her life then spiraled downward. She began drinking too much and became angry and argumentative. She was broke and friendless.

In *The Match*, author Frost says, "Of all the wealthy and privileged friends around the world whom she'd treated with such generosity and warmth throughout her life, only her former employer at Pebble Beach, Samuel Morse, stepped forward to help. He saw to it that Marion was moved back to Pebble Beach and gave her a house, rent-free, and a face-saving title with no actual responsibilities at his Del Monte Properties Company."

She died in a nursing home in Pacific Grove in 1944.

Friendships

Sam based his friendships around activities. He had friends in the clubs with whom he played golf or discussed political machinations, friends with whom he painted, boxed, sailed, rode, drank or danced with their wives. He played team sports well and was generally a good athlete. He was extremely loyal to his friends no matter what their situation.

Many claimed the distinction of being Sam's close friend and he would say the same of them. In his first memoir, I counted over 30 "my good friend" descriptions from Charlie Chaplin and Earl Warren to Frank McComas and Jo Mora. He liked to let down his hair with cowboys, politicians, dukes, and stars. He could sail, ride, shoot, box, write and paint, and he had good friends to do those things with him. He liked to be in a crowd and thrived on the electricity of groups.

Sam liked people and pretty much everyone liked him. He did have enemies but they didn't seem to hold their enmity. In his cowboy days, the killer Mac backed down from a fight, and in the next instant asked for a job. General Hubbard and his man A.D. Sheppard initiated Sam's Del Monte career with a full pitched battle to get him fired yet eventually realized it was better to help than antagonize him.

We know Sam wanted to see people have a good time and not just so he could sell lots in Pebble Beach. His charm was in his straightforward nature, good humor and great storytelling. His acumen in business was learned from Hammond and Crocker and other leaders of the time. He knew how to do things right and with class and style. He also knew how to manage employees and how to strike a good deal.

Sam's intense loyalty to his friends and employees was a major attribute. Marion Hollins is just one example. He gave a piece of land to the artist Jo Mora for building a home and commissioned several pieces from him. The last sculpture Mora did was a small statue of Sam that sits in my living room. It is dedicated to "My friend Sam Morse with esteem," dated 1944. When Sam's friend and partner Herbert Fleishhacker went bust in the '30s, Sam gave him a fair price for his stock and kept him on the board of directors, despite the disgrace surrounding the banker.

L: Cartoon by Jo Mora, undated
R: Small statue of Sam by Mora 1930

1929

1929 started out well in terms of investments. Sam sailed the beautiful yacht The *Temptress* to Tahiti in the spring, then sold her, as he had no further sailing intentions, which turned out to be a lucky investment choice, for the Depression ended a lot of frivolity and the boat would have had to be scuttled. He told the story of a friend of his who worked at U.S. Steel. Sam admired the man and bought a sizeable position in the company. In mid-1929 the man was fired for reasons Sam did not agree with and he sold his stock in a fit of spite. Of course, it was near the top of the market and Sam made a tidy profit. Another good investment.

The Roaring Twenties closed with a bang. The stock market crash in October was a harbinger of the Depression to follow. It was not immediately evident, but hotel rooms showed more vacancies, lot sales slowed and there were fewer applications for memberships to join the clubs. Fortunately, Sam had the sand plant and the water company with steady revenues.

Chapter Eighteen

The Great Depression

Sam Morse's empire was in trouble. His Del Monte Properties lost money each year of the Great Depression. The hotels were practically empty, and the golf clubs on the verge of closing. Lot sales in Pebble Beach were moribund. The sand plant and the water company were the only profitable enterprises and just barely. What Sam worked so hard to create was coming apart.

After the stock market crash in '29, business carried on as usual for a while. Beautiful people came to the hotel and the staff made sure they were photographed and the pictures made it into magazines and newspapers. Some people kept their money and others kept up their appearances. Sam kept necessary and appropriate staff, and he made sure his dining room was full. Freddy Stanley, son of the manager Carl Stanley, said at one point the hotel had 100 gardeners and two guests.

An amusing story recounts the tale of James W. Perry, whose large home was on the 1st fairway of Pebble Beach (now Casa Palmero). He was a stock and bond man who lost everything in the crash and subsequent decline in the market. His wife left him and he lived alone in the big house. The company took over ownership of the property but allowed him to continue to live there; there really was no market for those big houses in the '30s, and Sam saw no reason to evict the poor fellow. Sam wrote to Perry and said he needed to keep the dining room looking busy and would he mind eating dinner there on occasion as his guest. Perry still had elegant clothes and could look well off, although he wasn't. Of course, he understood this was a kindness and not a necessity, but he readily accepted the offer. He wrote back to Sam and agreed but asked if he could include a martini, as he liked to have a martini before dinner. Sam told him to have two martinis.

It was clear the economy was not improving soon and guest visits to the hotel and Lodge were declining, but Sam never gave up. Even at the bottom, when he sold the water company to raise much-needed cash, he continued to offer top-tier service and the business appeared to be doing well. In many ways he benefitted from the Depression.

Two occurrences allowed him to expand his empire and his control of it. The first concerned his partner Herbert Fleishhacker.

Fleishhacker Redux

Time Magazine ran the following story in 1938:

In San Francisco a municipal swimming pool, zoo and park all bear the name of Fleishhacker—not only because Banker Herbert Fleishhacker was a big contributor to them, but because when serving a brief term as a park commissioner he named almost everything but the city sidewalks after himself. Generally regarded as the West Coast's No. 2 financier (Amadeo Peter Giannini, No. 1), Herbert Fleishhacker for years has headed Anglo California National Bank, seen its deposits zoom from $4,500,000 to $200,000,000. Last week his career as a banker was over.

A raucously indefatigable practical joker (he once planted 100 pigeons in a friend's office), heavy-jowled, big-nosed Herbert got into banking in 1907 after making a small fortune in wood, paper, and power mills. Subsequent huge profits in shipping, agriculture, oil, mining, hotels and cement won him great repute as a daring plunger. But some stockholders charged that his plunges were more profitable to Herbert than to them. (Last month the Maritime Commission listed him among those who milked the Dollar Line almost to extinction.)

Last year a San Francisco judge found him guilty of pocketing emoluments of some $300,000 from a loan his bank made to a firm reselling Government steel after the War (TIME, Sept. 6, 1937, et seq.). This year another judge ordered him to pay damages of $651,579 for selling at too low a price some oil lands belonging to certain Lazard Frères heirs in 1915-17. Although he has appealed both cases, Herbert Fleishhacker last week cited them in turning in his resignation. "I feel," said he, "that the best interests of the bank may be prejudiced by my serving as president..." When judgments of $736,485 were returned against him in the Government steel case last March, he was granted a 60-day stay provided he post $800,000 bond. He failed to post it — presumably because he could not raise the money — and the court started attaching his assets in August. Last week Herbert made a date for November 10 to list his assets before a referee in bankruptcy, and turned management of the bank over to his less flamboyant brother Mortimer.

It is a speculation but possible that the cash for the down payment in 1919 for Del Monte was from these emoluments. The amounts are the same and the timing is perfect. It was his personal cash, not from the bank, and although he was rich, $300,000 was a lot of money.

Fleishhacker's need for cash provided Sam with a way to help his friend (and himself). He bought out Fleishhacker's interest in the company but kept him as a board member. Fleishhacker was much relieved. Although the amount he paid for the shares is not known, Sam declared it a fair price. Fleishhacker must have thought so too as they remained friends throughout the rest of his life.

Another benefit to Sam during the Depression was his ability to buy out the Jacks sisters. These two spinsters were the last members of the Jacks family living in California. Perhaps because of the local antipathy towards their father, David Jacks, the two of them moved to Palo Alto. Sam tried to buy their property for years as he was leasing part of it for the golf course. Deals appeared to be made only to be broken off at the last minute. But in 1936 they finally agreed to a price. Sam blamed their agent for the difficulties and when the sisters brought in new agent, Colbert Coldwell, they agreed on a price. Sam had a high opinion of Coldwell and was grateful he could arrange the deal with the Jacks.(Coldwell went on to found Coldwell Banker, an extremely successful agency). Now Sam needed to get the money.

He sold the water company to keep the hotel and golf operations alive, but now he needed close to $1,000,000, which in the middle of the Depression was a great deal of money. The Jacks and Fleishhacker were waiting to be paid. He raised cash twice before, once when he was buying the operation and then after the fire. Both bonds were repaid in a timely manner, and he figured his good reputation (and the good publicity he generated) would help him. He was right. In a relatively short time he sold a new bond issue to a consortium of insurance companies. He acquired Rancho Aguajito from the Jacks and gave Herbert his much-needed cash. The need to repay the loan weighed on him and he cut personal expenses wherever he could. His daughter, Mary, said they moved out of the "President's House" in order to use it as part of the Lodge operation and they moved into the hotel, where there were plenty of rooms available.

Publicity Helps

When business faltered during the Depression, Sam went into high gear. When other operators folded up shop, he did everything to keep going and keep up appearances. When he was desperate for cash, he quietly sold the Monterey Water Works, saying afterward that the community should own the water. He actually sold it to a San Francisco corporation headed by the Lillienthal family. He did not want to appear needy so he made it sound benevolent. He was excellent at "making the story better." Part of the sale price was free water on his personal properties for 50 years. We were sad to see that go in 1987, but the River Ranch has a very productive well.

Sam's ability to put a favorable spin on his life and business helped him a great deal during the Depression, like when asked if he was related to the inventor of the telegraph: "All us Morses are related." The inventor happened to be a fifth cousin two times removed.

Sam made a promotional film depicting the beauty of the Monterey Peninsula. He took the film to Chicago and New York to present at travel agent conventions. The film, of course, included snapshots of movie stars, politicians and wealthy folks. He coined, or his publicist Herb Cerwin did, phrases such as "the most photographed tree in the world" about the Lone Cypress, still so dubbed by "Wikipedia." Also, it is said he coined the phrase, "the greatest meeting of land and sea," which he attributed to R. L. Stevenson. He never made a specific reference to one of Stevenson's books or travelogues because there were none. Either he or one of his friends, perhaps Francis McComas or Herb Cerwin, made it up.

Sam traveled to South America in 1932 on a trade mission. A group from California loaded a ship full of goods, equipment and brochures and visited Cuba, Cartegena, Columbia and other South American ports. The mission was a partial success but as the Depression wore on and trade slowed, so not much came of it. Sam, however, enjoyed the trip and felt it was worthwhile.

Sam at Sloppy Joe's Bar in Havana, Cuba

Movie Stars, etc.

Many movie stars came to the Hotel Del Monte or the Del Monte Lodge and Sam made sure the press knew about it. He knew how to fill up the rooms and did not mind getting photographed with the guests, especially politicians, sports stars and actresses. Charlie Chaplan became a good friend of Sam's as did movie mogul Sam Goldwyn. Others like Jean Harlow and William Powell stayed with him at River Ranch. Sam's blustery, sportsman's image coupled with an oversized personality was surely appealing to them all.

Despite his efforts, the hotel looked like it might fail. The war was breaking out in Europe and Sam thought this would make it even tougher. In fact, the opposite was true.

The Navy, 1938

As the war in Europe began to expand, the U.S. made preparations for our eventual involvement. Armaments were prepared and men were recruited. The Navy Air Force needed pilots and those pilots needed training. An admiral approached Sam about using his landing field and hotel as a flight training school. The field was part of the hotel but Sam had recently purchased 150 acres of land from T.A. Work which was better suited for an airport. He made 37 acres available to the Navy to build a standard "4" landing field, which became the civilian Monterey Airport at the end of the war.

The hotel suffered even more than the Lodge so Sam jumped at the idea of the Navy leasing the property. He could handle the regular guests at the Lodge and the new "Cottage Row" which increased the number of guest rooms.

Sam made a deal with the Navy to house 1,600 servicemen at the hotel and give them three meals a day for $5 a head. His chef was up for it and Sam reduced the room staff to the bare necessity and made a small operating profit. In 1947 he sold the old hotel and the land around it to the Navy for $2.5 million.

Sam also had another reason to move away from Monterey besides the low occupancy of the hotel. Cannery Row.

Cannery Row

"Carmel-by-the-Sea, Monterey-by-the-Smell, and Pacific Grove by God."

A well-known description of the first three towns on the Monterey Peninsula, to which you could add *Pebble Beach by Sam Morse.*

When Charles Crocker first discovered the benefits of a large luxury resort hotel in Monterey, the city consisted of a few adobes and small homes and a Chinese fishing village on the bay. The city had barely grown since then and the former state capital became a backwater. The missions were falling apart and the adobes crumbling. Robert Louis Stevenson famously fled the area after decrying the arrival of the "great caravansary."

Along Ocean View Avenue between Monterey and Pacific Grove, Hugh Tevis built a beautiful California ranch style mansion 1,000 feet long, with a bowling alley, stables, a pool and a 200-foot pier. It was a combination of one- and two-story buildings hugging the coast.

Hugh Tevis, son of Lloyd Tevis, one of the richest men in the U.S., had just married the beautiful and flirtatious Cornelia Baxter of Denver and while the house was under construction they took off for Japan on their honeymoon. He died there of a stomach ailment, leaving his widow very wealthy.

She never moved into their love nest and sold the property to a couple from Pittsburgh. The Murrays lived there for many years, but sold off pieces of the property.

The eventual buyers were the sardine canneries. Sardines were plentiful in Monterey Bay, and demand for them was strong before World War II through the early '60s. The canneries multiplied and they changed the name of Ocean View Boulevard to Cannery Row after John Steinbeck's book of the same name.

The stench from the canneries was horrific and the pollution in the bay, deadly. The hotel was near the canneries so guests often got a nauseating dead-fish odor mixed in with their grilled streaks. The heated salt water pool was unique at the time but the offal from the canneries found its way into the intake valves and the pool became unusable. Sam saw no way around the problems with the canneries and was happy to have the Navy take the property off his hands.

John Steinbeck began Cannery Row with this description:…"(it) is a poem, a stink, a grating noise, a quality of light, a tone, a habit, a nostalgia, a dream. Cannery Row is the gathered and the scattered, tin and iron and rust and splintered wood, chipped pavement and weedy lots and junk heaps, sardine canneries of corrugated iron, honkytonks, restaurants and whorehouses, and little crowded groceries, and laboratories and flophouses." Cannery Row was not exactly the neighbor for a luxury hotel.

In the 1950s when Sam was firmly ensconced in Pebble Beach and well away from the stench of

Cannery Row Madam
Flora Woods

Sam and Earl Warren

Cannery Row, he received a surprising phone call. Flora Woods, the famous madam and owner of the Lone Star Cafe on Cannery Row, began the call with, "Mr. Morse, I need your help." Flora was immortalized in Steinbeck's book as Dora Flood and the bar as The Golden Bear. Flora said the State of California wanted to take away her liquor license. She said, "You know I am providing an important service to Monterey. If my girls were not here, then the soldiers at Fort Ord would be after the local girls."

Sam thought for a moment and said, "Well Flora, I am not sure what I can do, but I'll make a few calls."

His first and only call was to Governor

Earl Warren, a friend of Sam's. Sam explained the situation and Governor Warren said, "Well I'm not sure what I can do, but I'll make a few calls."

A week later Flora was back on the line, "Mr. Morse, I don't know what you did, but thank you very much. The state is allowing me to keep my liquor license."

Tevis Family

Hugh Tevis, builder of the original mansion on Cannery Row, was not the last Tevis in Monterey. Other descendants of his father, Lloyd, live there today. The Tevis family story is interesting as it is a classic example of spoiled wealth.

Lloyd Tevis, Senior, was a financier who, among other things, bankrolled George Hearst, the famous mining engineer and father of William Randolph Hearst. They engineered a takeover of Wells Fargo and Tevis was president for twenty years. Tevis had holdings amounting to 300,000 acres in Kern County and formed the land company of that name. He acquired this vast acreage through the Desert Reclamation Act (DRA). The DRA was conceived as a way to develop desert land. The way Tevis used it was legal but just barely. Before the act became law he had vagrants file claims in case the government decided to sell the desert land. Through their contacts in government, Tevis and his people were the first to find out about the DRA. They collected all the claims from the vagrants and other functionaries and exercised the options. The Tevis place was the second largest ranch in California after Henry Miller's.

Tevis was one of the first to have a mansion on Nob Hill at 1316 Taylor Street. He and his sons also had mansions at Lake Tahoe, Marin, Monterey, Los Gatos, and more. He left his estate to his wife, Susan, who, when she died in 1902, left it to her three surviving children but pointedly nothing to the widow of Hugh Tevis. Susan's estate was valued at $51,500,000, a vast amount at the time.

Unfortunately, his surviving son, William (Bill) Saunders Tevis, made some seriously bad investments including an attempt to start a regional railroad to serve the San Francisco Bay. Their family story told to me by his grandson Richard (Dick) Tevis, goes like this:

Bill Tevis married the daughter of Romualdo Pacheco, the only Mexican-American governor of California. With these two-strong willed and successful men as role models, Bill Tevis decided he had to make his mark on the world. This seems to be a common trait among the sons of the rich. They want to prove their mettle in business, but do not have the acumen. The result is often disastrous. He should have just lived off his substantial income.

Tevis decided a regional transit system serving Oakland, Fremont, San Jose and San Mateo as well as San Francisco would be a good idea. Starting in 1910, he began acquiring property and building rights to complete the plan. Oakland boomed in the period after the earthquake and he calculated a railroad bridge connecting it to San Francisco would be highly profitable. He kept a great deal of gold in banks in

England. He used this gold as loan security to buy the land and to pay for architects and engineers to build the rail system. This was a very expensive project. In essence, he planned to build the first Bay Area Rapid Transit or BART system. Today BART moves tens of thousands of commuters daily, and runs up and down the East Bay and the San Francisco Peninsula.

As his plans came along, World War I broke out, causing a massive problem for young Tevis, whose cash ran low with all the commitments he made and creditors were getting nervous. He wanted to get his gold out of England but that country, like others in Europe, stopped all gold movement or sale as a wartime measure. Tevis was in trouble. His "BART" system went bankrupt. According to Dick, his father, Lloyd, son of Bill, was traveling by private rail car around Europe when he got the news about the family misfortune. Dick said the he "went from being the richest, most eligible bachelor in California to the least eligible."

Dick Tevis was a charming man and by no means a pauper. He showed me his portfolio once when he was considering hiring my firm for money management. (He decided I would just want to sell things and he wouldn't get those lovely dividend checks in his mailbox any longer, so I didn't get the business.) He died in 2000, the year there was no inheritance tax, leaving a good-sized tax-free estate to his children. His children, John and Sheila, were very close to him and mourned his passing but applauded his timing. The house near the Carmel Mission stayed in the family through the hard times into the 1950s.

The Depression dragged on in the United States as Europe was preparing to go to war but in a way Hotel Del Monte benefitted from these tough times. People stopped going to Europe for vacations due to the war and Sam's push on publicity reached them. Getting far away from Europe was appealing. Two of those people were Salvador Dali and his wife, Gala.

The Dali Party

In late 1939 Fortune Magazine published an interview with Sam, with glossy color photos of the rich and famous arriving at the hotel or Lodge. Sam did not like the finished interview, perhaps because they called his dream a failure and said he was a poor dresser, wearing "ill-fitting tweeds." However, the scenery laid out in the pictures was compelling. The Lone Cypress, Pebble Beach Golf Links, famous names and the mansions of the wealthy were alluring to many. The article attracted a lot of attention and may have been the trigger for Dali's arrival in Del Monte.

Salvador Dali and his wife, Gala, stayed in the Del Monte Lodge Cottage Row in Pebble Beach on and off from 1940 to 1948, becoming somewhat friendly with the local citizenry. He joined the Carmel Art Association and the couple entertained at the hotel or the Lodge. He refused to speak English, of which he was perfectly capable, but insisted on French or Spanish.

SAMUEL F. B. MORSE, DEL MONTE'S HEAD MAN

64

Photo from the 1939 *Fortune Magazine* interview

In Sam's opinion, Dali was a fine classical painter but could not make much of a living doing it. Gala was from "somewhere north of the Caspian, a Tartar, I believe," said Sam, and she influenced Dali significantly. Sam said, "His mustache grew longer and was waxed more professionally and his style changed. Surrealism became their school of choice."

The Depression flattened income disparity, and the war continued that trend. Still, there were many wealthy people with the time and cash for a trip to Del Monte. Just as in earlier days when fiction writers glamorized California, publicist Herb Cerwin made sure East Coasters knew Del Monte was alive and welcoming. He placed movie star pictures in papers around the country and people loved it. Maybe for the same reason Monopoly became popular at the time: people who could never afford it enjoyed reading about who's who in Game and Gossip, the publicity rag for Del Monte.

With Dali in residence, Cerwin came up with a new idea to get public attention -- a surrealists' party hosted by Dali. Dali was amenable to the idea and Gala, who loved being in the public eye, supported him enthusiastically.

The Navy occupied the hotel at the time, but Dali took over the "Bali" room for the party. He hired local artist and John Steinbeck's bosom buddy Bruce Ariss as his set designer. The "surrealists" would be dining in the forest, so they filled the entire room with papier maché trees and bushes, the waiters wore bizarre animal costumes and Dali and Gala were seated at the end of the head table appearing to be sitting up in bed. She fed a lion cub from a baby bottle and live frogs were served as a pretend main course.

At the foot of the main table and a few feet behind was a ruined car with a naked girl inside appearing to be dead. Ariss later explained he had given the model several sleeping pills and she slept through the entire event, but he worried about fire with all the paper decorations and how he could rescue the girl should it become necessary.

Mary Morse was seated at the end of the table with her date, John Haffner. Behind her was the wrecked car and people kept bumping into Mary trying to get a picture

Gala and Dali in costume at the party

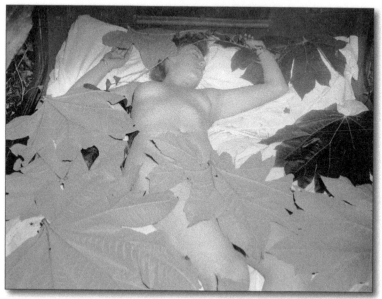

Nude model in the wrecked car

of the nude girl. Mary said she did not like the party at all. She did not enjoy competing for attention with a naked girl.

Nancy Morse and Bob Hope

The party, a fundraiser for needy artists, had several celebrity guests including Bob Hope, Jackie Coogan, and Gloria Vanderbilt. The Del Monte press machine went into high gear to get the word out. Articles appeared about it off and on, including one in the New Yorker 70 years later in 2011. A YouTube video entitled "Dali's Dizzy Dinner" features Hope opening the frog platter.

In Sam's words, "I have attended a lot of parties in my life… but this one topped them all. It would not have surprised me at all if someone brought in a platter with a bleeding head on it and Salome danced vigorously with nothing on but the last veil."

He talked about the wild parties at the Carmel Art Association. It is tempting to remind the current members of the time when their staid organization presented a completely nude woman on a platter held up by four "blackamoors." Back then, the Art Association also auctioned off a group of nude women in a "slave market."

Sam was a firm believer in free publicity and although the party was expensive it created a tremendous buzz. Many people wanted to come and would have paid the $500 admission to join in but it was sold out. Sam spent $50,000 on the party, well over the contributions, but the expenses were covered eventually by the increase in occupancy created by the publicity.

The extravaganza in June 1941 was the last time Hotel Del Monte hosted a large party. By the end of the year, the U.S. was pulled into the war and the Navy took over the hotel entirely. The main building with the dining room is now called Hermann Hall. The 160 acres of gardens have been seriously reduced. The swimming pavilion burned down in 1930 and was not replaced. Several military style buildings now crowd the property. The main building still displays its former glory with high ceilings, beautiful murals by Frank McComas and others and highly polished Spanish tiles on the floor. Once a year it displays a touch of its former glamour when the Navy holds a winter fundraising ball with attendees in formal attire: men in dress blues, women in ball gowns.

The railroad line was discontinued in the 1960s and the nascent town of Del Monte ceased to exist. But it was not the end of the line for Sam Morse or his artistic dream of Del Monte.

Chapter Nineteen

The Artist, The Investor, and The Brawler

Some people believe Sam was just an investor-developer which is far from accurate. In fact, he was not a very good investor and did not amass a great fortune. He cared about little beyond what gave him the means to enjoy his life. He dived into everything with gusto and creativity. One of those passions was painting, a very common pastime on the Monterey Peninsula.

Carmel

Starting in the 1910s the art scene on the Monterey Peninsula was robust and Carmel was the reason. The town was designed by its founders to be an artists' community. Frank Power's wife, Jane Gallatin Powers, was an artist and loved to come down from San Francisco to the little hotel above the Carmel Beach to draw and paint. In 1916 Powers and his friend Frank Devendorf bought the hotel and all the land around it and laid out a plan to build smaller houses just for artists and weekenders. The bohemian community grew quickly and Carmel became well known as a quirky and entertaining town. An outdoor theater was constructed, parties with large bonfires were held on the beach and it was generally a very convivial time. Painters included Rollo Peters, John Shea, Ted Criley, Armand Hanson, Paul Whitman, Frank and Gene McComas, and hundreds of seascapers. Photographers Edward Weston, Wynn Bullock, and later Ansel Adams lived on the peninsula or just down the coast in the Carmel Highlands.

Well known writers who visited or lived there include Jack London, Sinclair Lewis (a classmate of Sam's at Yale), Robinson Jeffers and others. The most famous writer, Robert Louis Stevenson, did not live in Carmel. It didn't exist in his time. He lived in Monterey and left when the Hotel Del Monte was built. Author, Henry Miller arrived later and secluded himself in the mountains of Big Sur.

Sam caught the art bug and worked in charcoal, continuing to paint and draw for the rest of his life. He was fascinated with the Cypress trees growing along the coast, with names like the Ghost Tree and the Witch Tree and the Lone Cypress. He painted of all of those, but the Lone Cypress was his favorite. Later he took up water colors and painted landscapes. He was quite prolific for a busy man and even lent one of his signed paintings for use on a much-reproduced Kurok tray. His third wife, Maurine, disposed of most of his works or gave them to her fourth husband, Milton Coburn. Sam, like many men of his generation (Eisenhower, Churchill, even Hitler) found painting to be a welcome distraction.

His mother was also an artist and Sam inherited her sense of color, design and balance. She may also have given him some training in technique. The environment of the Monterey

Sam at his easel, c.1960

Peninsula also was a significant contributor to his art muscles. Not only the spectacular scenery, but the art community was attractive. His closest friend was artist Frank McComas, who helped Sam lay out some of the landscaping in Pebble Beach.

He thought of land development as an artist thinks of a canvas. He often consulted with artists on landscaping, golf course design and home building. McComas was involved in many of these projects as well as murals in the hotel and lodge. McComas was an original member of the Cypress Point Club and helped design the course.

Sam told me that if I went into business I should make sure I had art in my life, because that would provide me the right balance I needed to be successful.

The Investor

I was upset to see reference to Sam at the Carmel Valley History Center as one of a group of investors who bought Carmel Valley. I couldn't disagree more. Although Sam was indeed involved in buying vast acreage in Carmel Valley, he was more artist than investor. He was too specific about where he would invest, land on the Monterey Peninsula or the Carmel Valley. He said giving land for a fire station was the best investment he ever made, because they were now closer to his house. He bought stock in U.S. Steel because a friend worked there, and he sold it when his friend was fired. He made a profit, but it was the Roaring Twenties and everyone made profits. Or selling his yacht in late 1929; it wasn't an investment move, he had lost interest in ocean cruising. His purchase of 150 gallons of green whiskey just before Prohibition was another of his "great investments," but in this case, his profit was the reward of many friends when the casks were opened. Other "investments" included giving land to hospitals and schools. These altruistic investments were for his and the community's future, not for his own financial gain, although he may have benefited in some fashion.

If he was a good investor he would have grown his empire and branched out beyond the local level instead of what he did: nurture his local property. He once had a good opportunity to expand with an offer from the Hotel Del Coronado, but he backed out of the deal.

He still had investments in the Pacific Improvement Company to look after, but they were not his and his sole job was to sell them. The big Crocker-Huffman Ranch was sold and the property at Castle Crags given to the state. Hope Ranch in California was developed by others although Sam had the chance to do that, too, but he was married to the Monterey Peninsula and he did not want to have an affair with Santa Barbara or San Diego.

Then again, artists typically are not good investors. They love their work too much and given the choice, would hold onto every piece created. Since Sam's art for the first part of his life was the development of the Peninsula, he had to let it go, parcel by parcel. This was exactly as he had planned. He reviewed every home design from where the house would sit on the lot to the architectural style. There was no zoning regulation or enforcement in Pebble Beach until after he died. The county seemed to know that he would not let the place look haphazard or derelict.

Sam loved the Monterey Peninsula like an artist loves his paintings. He was obsessed with making the peninsula perfect or at least his version of perfect. He made half-hearted attempts to buy other properties, like the Hotel Del Coronado, but they never amounted to much.

His portfolio of stocks was bland and he owned very little real estate on a personal level outside of his home and ranch. In fact, he did not even have a home in his name in Pebble Beach until he married Maurine. Then they lived in her house and only in 1955 did he build a personal residence. The 16,000-square-foot Japanese style home sits on the 1st fairway of the Pebble Beach golf links. The cost of the construction was $400,000. It has a fortress-like wall supporting a terrace connected to the living room that looks out over the golf course. The wall was great fun to climb as a young boy, but I never got to surprise Boss after climbing it. He was rarely home. My sister, Ellen told me that she would go across the course to use his over-heated indoor pool. In the little studio next to the pool were three TV sets tuned to different football games.

His friends included great investors from Bernard Baruch and Harold Mack to Charles Blythe and Dean Witter. Their expertise did not rub off on Sam. He was a board member of Crocker Bank and cozy with several big insurance companies that financed him, yet he only dealt with land in Monterey. He had the contacts and the brains but clearly not the ambition.

Some may argue that he made one very good investment and stopped there. That is probably true, too. Maybe he would not rank as a great investor, but he does rank as a great developer.

The Brawler

$\mathcal{S}$am never backed away from a fight. For him, it was part of being a man. He grew up with a soldier/lawyer father and a brother who was "the strongest man I knew." He was extremely strong himself and liked to show off at parties by ripping phone books in half. Sam kept in good shape and when he could find a sparring partner, he boxed. This was not always possible, so even into his 50s he went over to Seaside bars where soldiers from Fort Ord liked to hang out. Inevitably a fight broke out and Sam would dive in. For him it was great fun. His Boston accent and a fake lisp could invite trouble and he was ready for it.

During WWII taxis were scarce in San Francisco. Toward the end of the war, Sam and my father, Richard, were in the city. Richard was in the Navy and had seen action in the Pacific and was being reassigned to the O.S.S., the predecessor to the C.I.A. Sam hailed one of those hard-to-find cabs and it pulled to the curb in front of them. As Richard opened the door for Sam a man jumped in the cab and tried to pull the door shut. Sam reached in, grabbed the man by the scruff of his neck, and deposited him on the sidewalk, saying simply, "That's my cab." He was 60.

There is a persistent story still circulating at posh clubs in and around San Francisco that Sam once picked a fight with the wrong man, Cyril Tobin. Tobin was a scion of the family who owned the Hibernia Bank. Tobin, known to be a rather nasty fellow who could back it up with his fists, was not a large man but boxed at Harvard as Sam had at Yale. Sam was larger but maybe had had more to drink, when Tobin "took him to the woodshed" at a party at the Burlingame Country Club. Of course the family denies this was possible. On other occasions, Sam came home clearly looking like he had been in a fight. His only comment to his wife and daughter was that people didn't understand him.

This rollicking lifestyle did not fit well with Relda. She began to drink heavily and avoided friends and family. My father's brother Erik tells of a time he was on leave from Army training in San Francisco in 1946 and was invited to stay with the Morses. Richard and Mary (pregnant with yours truly) were in Ithaca where Richard studied hotel management at Cornell. Erik arrived at the President's House at Del Monte Lodge where Sam and Relda lived to find his brother's mother-in-law incapacitated and quite unprepared for his visit. He called up Stuyvie Fish, Richard's Harvard roommate, who lived nearby. They left Relda in bed and Erik went with Stuyvie to the Palo Corona Ranch in Carmel.

When Erik told me this story, he added another. That night the two bachelors went to dinner. Stuyvie's date was Ann Sothern, the beautiful blond movie star. They ate at Fandango, the only place in Pacific Grove serving wine. They were having a splendid evening when Erik saw his commanding officer a few tables away. They didn't exchange greetings, and when Erik went back to San Francisco the C.O. called him over and asked, "Was that Ann Sothern I saw you with Saturday night?" Erik, a typically droll New Englander, nonchalantly replied, "Yes," without explanation or elaboration. The captain apparently wanted details, or was upset about not being introduced, but, either way, he was tough on Erik thereafter.

Relda's alcoholism finally got the better of her and she died of heart failure on November 2, 1951, just before her 63rd birthday. Sam loved her dearly but had no idea how to help her. He loved to drink and his large frame processed the alcohol smoothly. Relda, though, was a victim of Prohibition, where people would drink too much in private because you could not drink in public. Sam might have been thinking of Relda when he said that "before Prohibition you rarely saw a woman drunk in public."

Chapter Twenty

Family and Business
Sam Tries the Next Generation
John Boit (Jack) Morse

After his brother died, Jack became the male face of the next-generation. He went to work for his father and Del Monte in the late 1930s and again after the war.

Unlike his shy and retiring older brother, Jack was no shrinking violet. Big, boisterous, and foul-mouthed, Jack cut quite a figure. Unfortunately, because of his alcoholism, he was never taken seriously as a businessman. Sam took Jack under his wing and tried grooming him to take over the business but subconsciously Jack undermined that plan. A hare-brained proposal after a long liquid lunch with some cronies was the last straw. They marched up to Sam's office above the Lodge and presented Sam with a plan, something akin to a Social Olympics: games and sports primarily played by the wealthy. It seemed like a wonderful idea over cocktails and lunch. Sam, fed up with Jack's drinking, fired him then and there in front of his friend, Dick Tevis.

Jack stopped drinking and joined Alcoholics Anonymous. He gave speeches and interviews and tried hard to encourage others with similar issues to join AA. When he left Del Monte, he started painting and in today's vernacular, flipping houses. His paintings were bright and happy, somewhat abstract and large scale.

Jack's house-flipping was remarkable. He had his father's eye for real estate. His modus operandi was buying a large house of questionable design in a good location and remodeling it with his artist's eye. He maintained that cars should be away from the house and that nothing that smacked of work should be visible to a guest. He flipped houses in Napa, Pebble Beach, Carmel, Santa Fe, San Miguel de Allende, Mexico and more. He bought, fixed up and lived in them for a year or two and sold them and moved on. He claimed he earned a good living.

He remodeled the Macomber mansion in Pebble Beach located on a hill above Carmel Bay. When Jack moved into the house he was the first resident, 50 years after it was built. As told earlier, Kingsley Macomber was so upset with the U.S. Government for adopting Prohibition that he moved to Paris as the house was being completed and never moved back.

This impressive structure, made of rustic logs and containing a fireplace a 6-foot-tall person could stand in, was built in the early '20s during Prohibition, and contained a hidden bar as well as a balcony for an orchestra.

Jack did not buy it, but lived there in the late '60s and made a small portion of the house livable. He installed a library and a studio in one wing and renovated the kitchen, one bedroom and a bath, essentially making a cozy cottage inside a decaying mansion. He left the grounds alone. The overgrown forest on the property created a primeval feeling Jack enjoyed.

When the Macombers bought the 80 acre lot they agreed with Sam to never subdivide it while their house was standing. The company took over the property at some point, and mysteriously the house burned down in the '70s. The company sold it to J. Lohr who promptly subdivided it.

Jack died a Nelson Rockefeller death in Los Angeles at the relatively young age of 75, in the arms of two prostitutes. His ashes, like Sam's, are scattered at the River Ranch.

Sam and son Jack at River Ranch, early 1950s

Mary Grows Up

Sam was a self-centered fellow with one major exception: his daughter Mary, who was brought up as an only child. Her much older siblings were reared in Chicago by their mother and stepfather. There were few other children in Pebble Beach and she filled her time with golf and tennis, watching polo or riding Western at the River Ranch. Her few playmates included her nearby cousins, the daughters of Byington Ford, Relda's brother. Sam and Byington were good friends, and "By" was Sam's top salesman along with Marion Hollins and Harrison Godwin. By lived in Pebble Beach in a Julia Morgan house on the golf course and like Sam, had property in Carmel Valley. They both played for the Shamrocks baseball team of the Abalone League. By had three daughters, Mary Jane, Pat and Tommy. Mary Jane was close in age to Mary and the two were best friends, but as they grew older they drifted apart when Mary went away to school, first Dominican College then to Stanford.

Mary was very shy despite her accomplished nature and public persona. Once she told Sam she didn't think they would let her into the Bali Room at the hotel at age 11, so Sam made her a pass.

Richard

In June of 1943, Mary was working part time at a magazine and helping with the war effort in New York, when she married Richard Osborne. Her prior boyfriend, John Haffner, was killed early in the war and she moved to New York to start her own life away from Pebble Beach.

Richard met Mary on his first trip to California in the summer of 1941. He and his close friend S. Stuyvesant (Stuyvie) Fish were at Harvard together and in the same club. Richard stayed with Stuyvie at the Fish Ranch (Palo Corona) in Carmel, but the social hub of the area was the Lodge at Pebble Beach. Stuyvie arranged for Richard to go to an event there and sent him ahead. He told him, "When you come to the gate just yell, 'Morse,' and keep driving." This system still works today in a way: look like you belong in Pebble Beach and wave smugly and the guards will let you through.

Richard came from an old East Coast family and was dapper, charming and good looking. San Francisco Chronicle newspaper columnist Herb Caen said in his annual New Year's column that Richard was "the best turned out," while playboy socialite Matthew Kelly was the best looking. Richard said it should have been the other way around: six feet two with blue eyes and a mischievous grin, he was an attractive guy. An excellent gamesman, he was a candidate master in chess, a life master in bridge and was runner up in the Backgammon World Championships in 1964. He loved fly fishing and later in life, like Sam, he took up painting. He did well at Harvard and after the war (U.S. Navy in the South Pacific) he went to Cornell's Hotel School, the best of its kind in the country. He was fluent in Danish and spoke passable French, as he would say, "with a charming accent."

Richard's father, Lithgow, served as the U.S. ambassador to Norway during WWII. His father, Thomas Mott Osborne, was an industrialist who sold his company and became a noted prison reformer, even spending a week in Auburn Penitentiary to get a feel of the place. Richard's mother, Lillie Suzanne Frederika Emerentzia Raben-Levetzau, was a Danish countess. She grew up in a manor house called Aalholm in Lolland, Denmark. Her father was the Danish Foreign minister during WWI. Lillie was half American: her mother's parents were Bostonians who moved to Paris in 1850.

Sam and Relda gave Richard and Mary a party when they first arrived in Pebble Beach. Jack Morse remembers Sam's toast as follows:

"When I first heard of this wedding I was disturbed. My daughter was going to marry an Easterner. On top of that, he is a HARVARD man. His father is a Democrat, his grandfather spent time in prison, and his mother is an immigrant." Although it was all in the good humor of roasting, there was an edge there that surfaced years later.

Their first child, Susan, was born in Carmel in 1944. Their second child, your author, was born in Ithaca, N.Y., near Cornell. The young family planned to move to Mexico City where Richard had a job managing a hotel under construction, but the builders kept delaying the completion. Sam, thinking of keeping his favorite child closer than Mexico, offered Richard a temporary job running the Monterey Peninsula Country Club. The temporary employment lasted 20 years.

Richard became Sam's close confidant and worked at the company from 1947 to 1965, first as the manager of the country club, then the assistant to Murray Matthews, the controller, and then on to president and ultimately vice-chairman. He was clearly Sam's heir-apparent.

Richard had a significant say in company affairs and initiated several important changes, one of those the land lease restrictions. (In Pebble Beach the properties were not sold but leased for 100 years.) This arrangement allowed Sam the control of house design, businesses—none except for Del Monte's—and even who could live there. As mentioned earlier, his partner, Herbert Fleishhacker, inserted a clause in the deeds to exclude certain races. Richard had this clause removed in the 1960s.

Richard was also instrumental in the company's only merger. In 1962, he orchestrated a deal with Chicago-based Wedron Silica. The sand operation in Pebble Beach was winding down and that source of steady income was disappearing: you can only strip-mine so deep near the ocean before leaving an unsightly and wet hole. Real estate sales came and went but by this time the resort, although somewhat seasonal, was well established and quite profitable.

Wedron Silica was a mining operation run by Al Gawthrop and Tom Taylor. With the merger they gained control of about 20% of the Del Monte Properties stock which proved fatal to the longevity of Morse family control. After Sam died, his trust owned about 25% of the stock, Mary owned 20% (willed to her by her mother) and the public shareholders owned the remaining 35%. Not long after Sam died, Denver oilman Marvin Davis, through his control of 20th Century Fox, made an offer for the company. Wedron Silica accepted the offer as did the trustees of Sam's estate. Mary felt there was little choice but to go along. Davis quickly sold it to a Japanese businessman with a shady past who lost control and a second Japanese group took it over.

Eventually a group including actor Clint Eastwood, who makes his home on the Peninsula, Peter Ueberroth, the former Commissioner of Baseball who ran the successful 1984 Olympics, and the renowned golfer Arnold Palmer bought Pebble Beach. The ownership also includes a slew of golfers who paid $1,000,000 each for what became a good investment that included bragging rights and favored tee times on the golf course.

Richard was also instrumental in bringing the U.S. Open to Pebble Beach. At the time the United States Golf Association (USGA) only played the tournament on private club courses and Pebble Beach was, and is now, a public course. Sam and Richard tried to take Pebble private to meet the necessary requirement to land the Open. When they announced their intention, a great clamor ensued. In an interview with the San Francisco Chronicle, Richard was asked where non-members would play in Pebble Beach if the last public course there went private. He replied that we still have a public course here, The Peter Hay (nothing more than a little pitch and putt operation near the Lodge). He was hooted down and the company backed away from making Pebble private. The first Open arrived in 1972 after the USGA recognized that although not a private club, Pebble Beach was the finest golf course in the country.

In the turbulent 1960s, Richard discovered Big Sur and the free-spirited people who lived there. His politics were always opposite of Sam's. As Sam became more and more conservative, Richard went the other way. He became actively involved in a California proposition to repeal the Rumford Fair Housing Act, which disallowed sellers from discriminating based on race. If they didn't want to sell to an African-American then that was their choice. Sam did not like Richard's campaigning but was resigned to the inevitable. The two of them continued to work well together until a little later in that decade.

Richard was the next relative, after Jack, to feel the wrath of Sam, this time over a woman. In the mid '60s, Richard and Mary's marriage was rocky and Sam got wind of it. A prominent San Francisco socialite declared Richard publicly as her co-respondent in her divorce. Sam was furious. One week he talked about giving Richard options on his stock and the next week Richard was out the door.

Like his brother-in law, Jack, Richard tried painting and living the artist's life, but that didn't last long. In Las Vegas he tried cashing a check in a casino, which required filling out a form (no ATMs in those days). When it came to "occupation" he proudly filled in "artist." The casino would not take the check. He complained that he was a "rich artist," to no avail. He returned to Carmel and with his business partner, Billy Hudson, developed the successful Crossroads Shopping Center.

Richard and Mary divorced in 1968 and both quickly remarried, she to local architect, Will Shaw, and he to a dark-haired attractive socialite named Olga de Bottari Ames. I enjoyed both of my new stepparents and outwardly applauded my parents' new acts of freedom, but inside I knew it was a mistake and hoped they would get back together. Of course, they never did.

Chapter Twenty-One

The Post-War Years

During the war, Californians were nervous. The bombing of Pearl Harbor stuck in their mind, there were occasional attempts at long-range bombing with balloons by the Japanese and sporadic attacks along the coastline. The internment of Japanese-Americans was an extension of that deep fear.

The Depression and then the war leveled income disparity, but Del Monte did not lower its standards: service was as top notch as it could be, and "the right people" came to the Lodge. Still, there were not enough of them and Sam barely got by. He retained all the employees and keep the place looking tip-top, but it wasn't until a few years after the war that business picked up.

The war's end brought great jubilation across the country and a sigh of relief in California. Ironically, after Hiroshima, the sunsets were especially beautiful due to all the particulate matter in the atmosphere.

As the economy grew and people realized the Depression was over, the Lodge filled up and lots began to sell again. The 1920s were fun but nothing compared to what was coming. This was the beginning of Sam's second heyday. The first real launch of the new era was a golf tournament created by movie star and crooner, Bing Crosby.

The Crosby: Bing Crosby's Clambake

The Crosby Clambake was hosted by Bing for a few of his friends. The tournament grew, attracting more players including some professionals. Originally held in Palm Springs, Bing was looking for a better location. Ted Durein, a sportswriter for the Monterey Peninsula Herald, is credited for convincing his friend Crosby that Pebble Beach would be an excellent location for his tournament. Crosby had a home in Pebble Beach and loved the golf course, so it didn't take much convincing on Durein's part. The tournament was moved to Pebble in 1947. The combination of celebrities playing golf with pros in a beautiful setting was a major crowd pleaser. The tournament grew and grew.

The tournament was a USGA sanctioned professional and amateur (Pro-Am) event with a date slot at the beginning of the season, fine for Palm Springs, but January weather in Pebble Beach could be pretty miserable. Not so good for golf, but great for staying inside and drinking and partying -- the primary purpose of "The Clambake."

The tournament was unique and had its characters, from Ray Bolger to Bill Murray, who liked to joke and horse around on the course and please the crowds. Pros put up with it as the play was enjoyable and the prizes substantial. The top pros enjoyed the relaxed atmosphere until Tiger Woods decided it was beneath him. It used to be an all male affair, but now amateur women are included. Mary Morse was asked to be the first female, but declined.

Sam with Ed Sullivan
and Bing Crosby, 1950s

Crosby and Pebble Beach were a great draw: movie stars, business moguls, golf pros all mingled together in the Pro-Am. Parties every day for two weeks reached a crescendo in the final four days of the actual tournament. We kids were totally ignored during the Crosby, which was fine with us. We wandered around collecting autographs, ogling celebrities and taking part in the free party food.

Bing lived on the 14th fairway in a house I got to know well after he died, a lovely large modern home with a very attractive den looking out over the golf course and the ocean. My first girlfriend's parents bought it from the estate. Her father, Ted Talbot, was the scion of a lumber and shipping family originally from San Francisco. Their daughter, Pam, was not only beautiful but owned a vintage Jaguar which never seemed to run. However, while it was in her driveway, we could sit in it very comfortably and make out. A cartoonist named Jimmy Hatlo lived on one side of Crosby's house and on the other a Central Valley farm baron named Ralph Hammonds.

Richard and Mary, representing Pebble Beach, had taken over most of the entertaining from Sam by then. They lived in a mansion not far from the Lodge which the company eventually bought and turned into a spa, Casa Palmero. Many celebrities came to the parties there or at other homes and at the Indian Village.

In 1954, Mary was pregnant with her fourth child, Ellen. Her delivery date was during the Crosby but she had a responsibility to make sure people went to the right parties and events, so she multi-tasked and, almost to the last minute in her hospital room, she took calls about where the parties were and who was going.

As a bridge player, one of my favorite Crosby stories is about a bridge game in the 1960s where one well-known golfer with an army of followers liked to play at a dollar a point. Normal stakes today are closer to one penny a point and even at that level you can win or lose $50 in a sitting. "The golfer" came over to Casa Palmero after dinner and the four men (Richard, Roger Lapham Jr., Paul Miller and the unnamed golfer) played late into the night rotating partners and, well, it was a very profitable game for all but the golfer. Polite gamblers at private games do not say how much they win or lose, but this game had to be in the thousands of dollars.

One unfortunate Crosby story made it into the newspapers. In 1964 during the tournament, my parents were entertaining at their house when Richard received an urgent call from the Lodge about Frank Sinatra having a temper tantrum.

It seems Sinatra wanted dinner at a little after midnight and the kitchen was closed. He was rude and insistent, clearly not used to being turned down. The manager of the Lodge was at wit's end and finally put Frankie in touch with Richard. Sinatra was abusive and angry but Richard was calm and professional despite the insults. He had his own kitchen staff make up some sandwiches and grabbed a couple of bottles of champagne to soothe the irritated celebrity. He had no idea what waited for him.

It was a short walk from Casa Palmero to Sinatra's room where his "Rat Pack" gathered. When Richard walked in the door with his hands full Sinatra slugged him between the eyes so hard he broke two bones in his own hand. The champagne and sandwiches went flying, the Rat Pack stopped any further activity and both Richard and Sinatra went to the hospital. An infuriated Morse had Sinatra's clothes and belongings packed up and dumped at the hospital with a note saying he could never return to Pebble Beach. The press loved it but it was clearly embarrassing to all. Richard never commented on it publicly and Sinatra was banned from Pebble Beach and the golf tournament for life.

Jan. 20, 1964 clipping from the *San Francisco News Call Bulletin*, in the River Ranch scrapbook

This was an out-of-the-ordinary event: the Crosby was a good-natured gathering of great golfers, wealthy socialites and celebrities, with parties every day and evening. The company gave a picnic at the Indian Village and Sam as well as Richard and other locals had events at their homes. It was reasonably attended as golf tournaments go, but did not overcrowd the Peninsula as the Concours, or what the locals call Car Week, does today.

After Bing Crosby died the tournament continued, but his widow no longer wanted his name associated with it. It is now the AT&T Pebble Beach Pro-Am and is in the less stormy month of February. Without the Crosby luster the tournament seems less fun and more business, but the backdrop remains spectacular. It still features celebrities, top pro golfers and business types, and the invitation to play in it is a hot ticket. I am possibly prejudiced, but it is rather soulless these days.

The tournament lost some of its appeal when Tiger Woods stopped participating and it is no longer the biggest event in Pebble Beach: that distinction is now held by the Concours d'Elegance, although the annual Pebble Beach Food and Wine Festival is gaining popularity.

Still, Pebble Beach is famous for its golf. The first U.S. Open was held there three years after Sam died and three more since, the next scheduled for 2019 to celebrate the 100-year anniversary of the course. It is not easy or inexpensive to play golf at Pebble. The current rules are the minority owners, Lodge guests, Beach Club members and then residents have first priority. If there are any openings, you get the privilege of paying $500 in greens fees, $100 for your caddy and then, of course, there are the cocktails in the Tap Room.

The Concours d'Elegance

Sam loved big events and one of his brain children was a road race around the forest in Pebble Beach. At the time, racing was an aristocratic sport, very expensive and glamorous, and sponsorships had not been conceived. It fit his description of a classy event. Europeans dominated the races and many of them came from aristocratic families. The first race was in 1950, and the last one in Pebble Beach was in 1956 when Ernie McAfee was killed. The course was tight and twisty and lined with trees. There were hay bales set along the sides, but they did not stop a speeding car. McAfee slammed his Ferrari into a pine tree on turn No. 7. The race continued the next year at the Laguna Seca Race Track, a celebrated course on an old Ford Ord artillery range on Highway 68.

As an adjunct to the races, the Pebble Beach sponsored a car show, Concours d'Elegance. The first few shows were low-energy events attracting mostly local car nuts and featuring current models. The big U.S. automobile companies produced yearly updates, notably the growth of tailfins. Within a few years the focus at the Concours changed: vintage cars became the standard and the crowds grew. Today

Pebble Beach Road Races 1952

thousands of people flood the little Monterey Peninsula during Car Week. The events have spilled over to Carmel, Monterey, and Carmel Valley, but the main show is still in Pebble Beach.

The event is held in August on the 18th fairway. Tickets are $300 and the proceeds go to charity. In 2016, the Best of Show was a 1936 Lancia Pinin Farina Cabriolet.

The Concours delivers a mighty lift to local businesses and charities. The County of Monterey estimates that in 2016 visitors spent $53 million, booked 17,978 hotel rooms and the Concours was attended by 85,000 people. Tax revenues were $4.8 million and all net proceeds went to local charities through the Pebble Beach Foundation.*

From the Pebble Beach Foundation website:

This prestigious, invitation-only competition is not only a spectacle of beautiful motorcars; it also serves as a fundraiser for nearly 100 charities throughout the Monterey Peninsula.

The Pebble Beach Concours d'Elegance brings together our passion for cars with the opportunity to raise money for people in need. With the help of our generous donors and sponsors, as well as many volunteers, the 2016 Concours was able to raise more than $1.7 million for charity. This brings the total raised for charity to more than $23 million since the Concours began in 1950.

Through our primary charitable partner, the Pebble Beach Company Foundation, proceeds from the Pebble Beach Concours benefit 85 local charities. Several charities also benefit directly from our Concours Opportunity

Drawings as well as grants provided through the Foundation. Additional charities volunteer time and effort in exchange for donations, while other nonprofits benefit from the use of Concours infrastructure, such as tents, to host their own fundraisers.

Social Olympics

Sporting events at Pebble Beach were geared toward the affluent and well-connected: yacht races, equestrian events including polo, tennis and celebrities to teach the game and a place to shoot trap. In the mid-'70s, a childhood friend of Mary's, Dick Tevis, a creative type who wrote books, dabbled in painting and told great stories, handled public relations for Del Monte

Dick introduced his idea for a series of games called "The Social Olympics" a few years earlier through Jack Morse and Sam had rejected it, but Sam was gone by then, so Dick gave it another go. The decathlon consisted of backgammon, bridge, polo, skeet shooting, dressage, tennis, golf, archery, fly fishing and sailing. It was an amusing idea, as most of Dick's were. The first (and only) leg of the decathlon was backgammon.

Backgammon, an ancient game in and out of popularity over the years, was big in the 70s. The tournament, held twice, was attended by world-class players and the social set. Your author played one game against the world champion, Oswald Jacoby and lost a small amount of money, but retained bragging rights for life. Another champion and author, Barclay Cooke, autographed his book for me... saying that if I had any technique at all and half my old man's nerve, I would be a champion.

Stuyvie Fish caught the tennis player Bobby Riggs cheating at the backgammon tournament. He stood up and declared, "You cheat!" and had Riggs thrown out.

The same day I asked Stuyvie where the smart money was and he pointed to his ranch looming over Carmel Bay, and said, "Up on that hill there." A gentleman who was listening said, "Oh, that's Ham Fish's place. I know him well." Stuyvie let him go on for a bit and then gently corrected him by saying Ham was his cousin. I stood by enjoying the scene. The gentleman's foot might still be in his mouth.

Backgammon lost its popularity by 1980 and The Social Olympics had a short life.

Local Events

The pet show, an annual small-scale local event, was held at the Lodge or at what is now Casa Palmero. The contestants brought their well-groomed canines, cats, ponies, ducks or goats and put them through their paces. The pet show was a rare event for the few children in Pebble Beach. In my era the only local children in Pebble Beach were the offspring of the car dealers, wealthy farmers, the idle rich and a few professionals. In summer the number expanded as the vacation homes were populated.

Communities

The separation of communities in Pebble Beach, the Country Club area, Carmel and Pacific Grove was a by-product of Sam's scheme to build a Newport of the West. Just as Carmel was created as an artist's community and Pacific Grove a Methodist Chautauqua, Sam saw Pebble Beach as a haven for wealthy sportsmen, California's social equivalent to tony retreats in the east and an alternative to the declining charm of Newport and Palm Beach. Although golf became the predominant sport, like sailing in Newport, golf was only part of the social scene. The children met at the stables for riding lessons, the Beach Club for sailing and swimming and at Gardiner's Tennis Ranch to learn the game.

John Gardiner came to Pebble Beach as a young man as the tennis pro. He told me that he was asked to be the coach of the Stanford football team, but Sam convinced him to stay at Pebble. That turned out well for them both. In the early 1960s he created the first Gardiner's Tennis Ranch in Carmel Valley and another in Scottsdale Arizona, both immensely popular while he was alive. He had summer tennis camps for children and luxurious rooms for adult guests. I attended the first camp and my youngest son, Ian, went to the last session 40 years later. When John's first wife passed away he married an Austrian woman who chose to close the children's camps in the 90s. Gardiner's Tennis Ranches went into steady decline and eventually closed.

Schools

For many years the only school in Pebble Beach was the Douglas School. Mary went there when Grace Douglas ran it, as did her daughter, Susan, but it closed after I attended second grade in 1954. The site is now the (Robert Louis) Stevenson School, an exclusive private prep and boarding school. I returned there in seventh grade.

Sam was interested in having an elite boarding school in Pebble Beach because he felt he owed his career to his schools, so he gave the land and some funds for the construction of "RLS." The school had growing pains in its early years and, in my time, was not a very good school: the teachers were mostly retired military men and other non-professionals. The boarding students were boys from San Francisco who could not get into better schools or were trouble makers. The headmaster, Robert Rickleffs, was caught skimming funds to feed his gambling habit and his best administrator left to head a competing school (York) in Monterey. Stevenson has grown considerably since then and is now well established as one of the better prep schools in California.

Sam the Wanderer

Sam was constantly on the move even into his final years. He just couldn't stay home. Besides his travels in the U.S. and abroad, he inspected his properties, visited with employees, and popped in on friends unannounced, often with celebrities in tow. He was often in the news thanks to his press machine and his love of people.

He brought celebrities around to meet his friends, from President Dwight Eisenhower and Walt Disney to Jean Harlow and Joan Fontaine. His friendships remained broad-based, though, and he kept up with all sorts of people during his life. My mother tells a story about driving up to the ranch with her father when he pulled off the road at Hitchcock Canyon and told her to wait in the car. When he returned 15 minutes later, he said that old Mr. Hitchcock lived alone and liked having someone visit and drink a glass of bourbon with him from time to time.

Sam with
Dwight Eisenhower

A constant refrain by my mother when I would ask for something was, "We're not rich." Then my friends would come over and be amazed by the mansion we lived in: ten bedrooms, eight bathrooms, and servants' quarters with a separate kitchen. In fifth grade my teacher at Junípero Serra School, the elementary school at the Mission, asked us each what our fathers did for a living. Most of the answers were pretty straightforward: doctors, electricians, plumbers, bankers. When it was my turn I had to confess I did not know. Everyone in the class laughed. I went home and asked my parents; they laughed, too. I didn't know what was so amusing. I knew my family controlled Pebble Beach, but what was their job? My father kindly explained to me that he was a developer.

I came to realize how important Sam was to the Peninsula in roundabout ways. Like at age 16 when a Pebble Beach policeman pulled me over for reckless driving, looked at my license and said, "If you do that again I will tell your parents."

Sidney Stuyvesant Fish

I've mentioned Stuyvie several times in this story, for he was a fixture in our family's life. He was a descendant of a famous New York family but he was a true Californian who moved here at age 5. His father, Sidney Webster Fish, and his mother, Olga Wiborg, moved west. Sidney's father was the head of the Illinois Central Railroad and his mother was a famous socialite. She was best known for her "400," a list of acceptable people in New York who could be invited to balls in the Gilded Age.

Stuyvie was a big hearty fellow who grew up in Carmel. Well over 6 feet tall, he was handsome with a broad chest and big smile. He was the man John Wayne wished he could be. Extremely friendly and hard drinking, he was a big hit at parties on the Peninsula. He went to the same primary and secondary schools as I did (Douglas and Cate School in Carpinteria), and then he went on to Harvard.

The *Atlantic Monthly's* story on his class reunion in October 1968 has a fun description of Mr. Fish:

> *Some of the rich classmates were keeping their pelf to themselves. There was, for example, Sidney Stuyvesant Fish, or Stuyvie as the other well-born and well-to-do called him. "Oh, Stuyvie, he's too awful, but he is nice," people would say as he appeared frolicking in the evening at the Hasty Pudding Club, dancing, dropping to one knee to kiss a lady's hand, and enjoying himself in the manner of one who has had a lifetime of practice. Stuyvie, it was generally felt, not only lacked a Harvard man's sense of social responsibility, he even lacked the pretense. "I sell a few hides to pay the taxes," he poor-mouthed, suggesting an improbable picture of himself in a dinner jacket leading a tallowy cow down a dusty arroyo to keep the sheriff from foreclosing on his splendid Palo Corona Ranch at Carmel, California.*

> *"I gave them some money, but not what they asked for," he said to prove he was a good fellow. "I'm fond of Harvard, but my feelings aren't gut-ripping, you know, and there are some people who are wondering if they should support the school if revolution is what they're learning here."*

> *"Stuyvie is a reactionary," said one of the classmates. But he is an amiable one, not given to angry kvetching, a twinkly-eyed bachelor who'd rather talk about pot-smoking escapades in Mexico, his efforts at preserving the California backland from suburban tractation, and the wild European boars he raises on his ranch and sells for a dollar fifty a pound. ("I have about two hundred of them, and they help to pay the taxes, too.") He ranks second in animal husbandry, however, because there is another classmate in Cedarburg, Wisconsin, who raises zebras, llamas, pygmy goats, addaxes, and wallabies.*

After college and the war Stuyvie went into mining for a brief period but when his father died he moved back to the Palo Corona. This ranch, which sits on a majestic hill above Carmel and Point Lobos, is possibly the most beautiful in California. Several-thousand-acres, it boasts redwood groves and forests as well as extensive pastures on the rolling hills below it. The iconic winding driveway up to the ranch house has been photographed and painted infinite times. The Fish family entertained guests from royalty (Princess Margaret) to artists (Dali) there for decades. The ranch is mostly a park now, although Stuyvie's widow Diana Fish still lives part time in the main house.

Stuyvie Fish (1920-1980) entertaining Princess Margaret (1925-2000)

Stuyvie was an eligible bachelor. His first marriage to Ginny Small didn't last long and there were no children. His second wife and widow, Diana Turner, also had no children. His closest relative was his first cousin Honore Murphy Donnelly, the daughter of Sarah Wiborg Murphy and Gerald Murphy of F. Scott Fitzgerald fame. Their mothers, Olga and Sarah Wiborg, were sisters. Honore's husband, Bill, was another entertaining gentleman. He was wounded in the war had a government job in the Department of the Interior. As he was a wounded vet, he was untouchable during administration changes. He liked to say that when the Democrats were in power he had a big corner office, but when the opposition took over, he was moved next to the broom closet. An unlikely but amusing anecdote. While Captain Donnelly was in Pebble Beach he ran the gun club located in the sand dunes on the north shore near Cypress Point. I was often drafted to load the skeet in a rickety shed not quite in their line of sight, but close. Alcohol was served.

Captain Donnelly had a favorite dinner party toast. He would stand up and say, "Here's to me…Good men are few." Wonderful fellow.

In 1947, Sam sold the hotel to the Navy and focused entirely on Pebble Beach and some work on the Jacks' Rancho Aguajito. He made a portion of it available for Monterey Peninsula College and on another portion in 1965 he built the Del Monte Shopping Center, the first of its kind on the Peninsula. He also set aside some parkland on the old Jacks' property and donated land to build the Community Hospital (CHOMP) and a fire station. In Pebble Beach, property sales were doing very well after the war, so Sam could focus on having a good time. Which he did.

Chapter Twenty-Two

Sam Remarries
Maurine Church Dalton Morse Coburn
(1894-1978)

After Relda died in 1951 Sam was single for a short time, during which he courted Joan Fontaine, but the woman he fell for was Maurine Church Dalton. Maurine was either twice widowed or twice divorced, or maybe one of each, I was never sure. Her last husband lived in Hawaii and she had a fondness for things Oriental. Her dog was Cho So, her house was designed in a Japanese style and her favorite store was Marsh's Oriental in Monterey. Their last house was a palace with a stone wall holding up a terrace that loomed over the 1st fairway of Pebble Beach. Maurine did not drive a Japanese car as they were not being imported then, so she settled for a Rolls Royce. Sam's last car was a Mustang.

Maurine was a very generous person, which I found out soon after they were married. For Christmas she gave us a generous cash gift, a $50 bill. For a kid who got 25 cents a week allowance, that was a lot of money. I remember one Christmas taking the $50

Sam marries Maurine Church Dalton
(1894-1978) in 1952 with grandchildren
in attendance

bill and going bowling with my friend Lawsy on Christmas day. We bowled for an hour and when I went to pay, they could not change the large bill… so the bowling was free.

Later in life Maurine became conservative and opinionated. In 1967, when I asked her what she thought of the Civil Rights movement, she said she wished someone would line up all those protesters and machine-gun them. Since I was a Civil Rights advocate and a Vietnam War protestor, her answer was not what I hoped for.

There is no doubt Sam was devoted to Maurine. After they were married, they were always together. He was near 70 when they got married, but he was a robust, hearty fellow and had plenty of life left in him. On their honeymoon they sailed up the Seine to Paris, then through canals to the Rhone and on to Marseille and Nice on a yacht called the *White Siren*. They stopped in villages on the way and found out what edible delicacies the locals were proud of and that would be part of their dinner that night. It was a glamorous leisurely trip I think would be fun to copy one day.

He bought another yacht in 1959, the *Vileehi* named after the prior owners Violet, Lee, and Hiram. After a year or so in California, they sailed her to the Mediterranean. She was a gorgeous schooner, 82-feet-long with the cabin located mid masts. I believe it is still for charter in Italy.

Sam continued his rounds into his 80s. He kept his office above the Lodge and visited with employees and friends who were around. He and Maurine drove around Pebble Beach or out to the valley and dropped in on friends and relatives. His overseas travel slowed down. He never liked flying much, he preferred the view from a car or train window.

After Sam died in 1969, Maurine remarried Milton (Mint) Coburn and lived in the same house where she had lived with Sam until she died and left the house to the Community Hospital of the Monterey Peninsula, which rented it out until they sold it. She was very involved with the hospital, especially the nursing program, and donated funds to build the nursing wing. She also started and donated many works to the well-regarded art collection that decorates the hospital walls.

Maurine left Mint all of Sam's personal things including his art, jewelry and collections. The family has no idea where much of this is now. We believe Mint sold most of it. Sam also left her a portion of the River Ranch. He gave Mary the main house, but he had wanted his own place there. Maurine immediately sold her house.

Maurine left a positive legacy on the Peninsula and is well known for endowing the nursing wing of Community Hospital and the school of nursing at Monterey Peninsula College, which is named after her. Her portrait is in the hospital entry area near Sam's, as the hospital's two most significant donors.

Sam had ten natural grandchildren. His oldest son, Sam Jr., died young, but had one child, Samuel III (Sammy3). Jack had two boys, Richardson (Rickie) and Peter. Nancy had two sons, Michael and Roderick Hooker, and one daughter, Anne (Jabby) Walker. I have three sisters, Susan, Polly and Ellen. Peter and Rod have passed away. The rest of us get along fine.

Sam left the remainder of his estate to Yale, Stevenson School and the Monterey Institute. My cousins enjoy the benefits of trust income as long as my mother is alive. They often ask about her health.

Chapter Twenty-Three

Advice to all

"If your feelings get hurt, it's your own damn fault," said Sam Morse to his sniffling 8-year-old-daughter, Mary. She remained guarded, and she passed that wisdom along to her children.

Sam loved to give advice. He truly felt he knew how to do things right and most of the time he did. Of course, there were failures, like when he decided to have sheep mow the golf course, or when he scraped seagull guano off the rocks for fertilizer. The sheep tore up the course in the first experiment and loud barking sea lions took over the rocks after they were scraped bare of guano. Also, the rocks looked awful, which upset Sam greatly, as he thought he had blighted nature. Both endeavors ended quickly. But, he also had a slew of winning ideas: rejuvenating the hotel, expanding the golf course, increasing the water supply and upscaling the plan for Pebble Beach.

He was specific about how he wanted things to look, much like an artist wants his painting to be perfect. In 1965, a new freeway extension of Highway One cut over the top of Carmel Hill through company property. Typically of Cal-Trans, they denuded the hill of all trees on both sides of the road. Sam instructed the forestry department to replant Monterey pine trees. Chief forester Otis Kadone, a meticulous man, planted the trees in a very orderly fashion, perfectly spaced in nice lines, like row crops.

When 80-year-old Sam came back from the River Ranch the following week, the first thing he did upon seeing the trees was to go over to the forestry department looking for Otis. "Where's Otis?" he bellowed. The fellows weren't sure, but they didn't want to say that to Mr. Morse. They said he was out inspecting the new trees. "Well you tell Otis he has to replant them. TREES DO NOT GROW IN A STRAIGHT LINE!!!"

In 1965, Sam was horrified to hear Humble Oil Company, a unit of Standard Oil, wanted to build a refinery on Monterey Bay. They picked a spot above the harbor where a rock crushing plant operated. The biggest polluters of the bay, the sardine canning industry, had finally wiped out the local fish and were closing one by one. Sam was delighted with this. Not only was the stink of dead fish horrific, but all the waste and offal was callously thrown into the bay. The canning industry was a major disaster for Monterey, and the only good thing that came out of it was the tourist industry springing up along Cannery Row years later.

Now a new potential threat to the bay loomed. The Humble Oil Company wanted a large refinery with a dock and port for loading crude and shipping finished products. The potential for spillage on top of the smog and visual issues bothered Sam enormously. He and other Peninsula residents including Fred Farr, the local State Senator, campaigned against the refinery. They had a petition signed by 15,000 people demanding the county not allow the refinery. But demographics in the county had changed and there were more people in the Salinas Valley now than on the Peninsula who wanted the jobs and industry a refinery would provide.

Initially the Monterey County Planning Commission denied a permit by a vote of three to two, but the developers appealed to the Board of Supervisors who overturned the Planning Commission ruling and gave a green light to the project. However, by this time Humble was getting the message and chose to build the plant in Benicia instead. The Benicians were and are happy to have it.

Sam liked to play kingmaker behind the scenes and often suggested certain people be appointed to specific jobs at the national and state levels. In a 1967 letter to Justin Dart, chairman of Dart Industries and a Republican insider, he recommended California Governor Ronald Reagan as Richard Nixon's running mate in the 1968 presidential election. Dart was on Reagan's "kitchen cabinet."

Sam often advised that "hard work and perseverance do not make you a success. If you stay in your office with your nose to the grindstone you are not out in the world, meeting the right people or expanding your life."

All Sam's cowboy and football stories had a moral of some kind. When he told me about bad man Mac MacFarlane's one-exit (the front door) cabin, the point was to always have an exit plan in any endeavor.

When Robert Trent Jones wanted to put the new golf course, Spyglass Hill, through the old Indian Village, Sam said no. He liked what was there and felt a need to preserve the Indian home site where they found a significant number of artifacts. There was a spring there and he conjectured the Indians used the place as a sort of spa. His version of conservation in this case was building some log cabins and tables and having picnics on the spot, but no development. The Pebble Beach Company now plans to develop the site.

Malcolm Millard, a local attorney now deceased, told me at the Old Capital Club in Monterey that Sam asked him if he was interested in running for the State Senate. Malcolm said yes in theory, but he would have to run against his law partner Fred Farr. "And that," said Malcolm, "was the end of my political career." Clearly he favored his friendship and partnership with Fred more than a potential political job. He also knew this was his one chance to get a statewide office: with the backing of Morse and his connections he had a good chance of winning. By turning him down he knew he would not be asked again.

I found a telegram from my father to Sam glued into a scrapbook at the ranch. Richard had "discovered" the *Idalia*, the ship that brought the Spanish explorer Viscaino to Monterey. She was in port in Europe and was for sale for $6,000. Richard was excited and knowing Sam loved history, suggested they buy it. Sam scornfully sent back a reply saying that if it really was Viscaino's ship it would be so rotten by now the sardines of Monterey Bay would swim right through the ship's hull.

Sam was nice to me but on one occasion I thought he was a little harsh. The pool at the ranch was built in the 1920s and had no

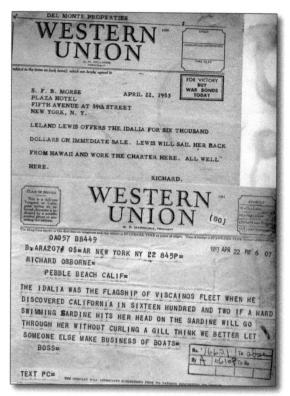

The telegram exchange regarding the *Idalia*

filter, meaning that at least once a summer we had to drain it and clean the scum off the bottom. When I was 15, my friend Ethan Russell (grandson of Helen Crocker Russell) and I were stuck with cleaning the pool. To our delight we discovered we could slide across the slime after a short running start. I was doing this when I hit a sticky spot, spun around and did a face plant on the cement.

I broke both front teeth. It hurt. When I saw my grandfather, he unsympathetically pointed out that if I had played football instead of soccer, I would have learned how to fall.

Chapter Twenty-Four

The Final Chapter

Sam Morse's indelible spirit permeates the Monterey Peninsula. His layout of Pebble Beach has proven timeless. He really did create the "Newport of the West." The golf courses, parks, statues, open spaces, and protected groves of trees are monuments to his vision and to his memory. He died May 10, 1969, just shy of his 84th birthday.

The various streets named after him as well as buildings and other honorifics show the love and respect felt by the people who knew him or experienced his work.

He often fought to ensure his dream was not marred. The man combined machismo with artistry, or as a friend of mine once said, "He had brains *and* balls." It took that to keep the state from putting a highway through Pebble Beach or to stop an oil company from building a refinery on Monterey Bay. He was a force for class and style by insisting on development that enhanced the natural beauty. He railed against the forces of ugly, tasteless growth. He did build the first major shopping center in the area but it had to be designed by famous architects Jack Warnecke and Lawrence Halperin. This was consistent with his philosophy. He wanted a growing vibrant community that met his criteria of both attractiveness and functionality.

The man liked to have a good time. He felt it was important to get out and be with people. He loved to play sports of all types from polo and football to tennis and golf. He worked out daily, swam often and took long sailing trips. He was also happy to join in a barroom brawl, nestle up to his Old Grand-Dad bourbon or try to get the attention of an attractive female. His art was important to him and his paintings adorn several public buildings, and stories about him, true and false, abound. He left most everything to local charities, as did Maurine, his third wife and widow.

For those who knew him, he will be remembered as a fine, fun-loving man who was fiercely loyal to his friends and employees. He played baseball with the Shamrocks in the Abalone League and the working people of Monterey. He went to beach bonfires with his artist friends and sang the Abalone song. He rode the range with his cowboys in the Central Valley; drank with the soldiers of Fort Ord; sailed to Tahiti from Pebble Beach; boxed with Kid McCoy; golfed and painted with President Eisenhower, and romanced Joan Fontaine at his ranch. After he married Maurine, they sailed up the Seine to Paris, then took canals and the Rhone River down to the Mediterranean to Marseille, where his father had died, and then on to Naples.

Sam Morse stopped the looting of the land on the Monterey Peninsula and saved it from the Cheaters, Liars and Thieves who came before him. He didn't want to follow their pattern of "build and bug out." He built the community around sports with the focus on golf, not sailing, like its east coast counterpart. He wanted to live in one of the most beautiful places on earth, play with his friends, and enjoy life. And he did.

When Sam died he left the bulk of his estate to educational institutions: Yale, Stevenson School, and the Monterey Institute of International Studies. His children were to receive the income until the last one died. Unfortunately tax laws changed in 1969, his trust was not updated and the estate was billed at the maximum rate. The trustees sold over 60 percent of his assets to raise the cash required. The sales included most of the acreage of his beloved River Ranch in Carmel Valley, which eventually became a park, but his daughter Mary kept the ranch house and a few acres around it.

His widow Maurine followed suit and left her estate including their house to the Community Hospital and is remembered as Maurine Church Coburn.

Sam represented the classic ideal of a masculine success story of his day. He was almost an archetype. He lived life on his terms. He worked hard and played hard, fraternizing with the rich, famous and influential while enjoying the company of others from all walks of life. He blended old and new, bridging the romantic notion of the cowboy days of the Old West and the modern man of enterprise. While by most standards he was wealthy, he wasn't greedy. In some ways, he was almost a model for enlightened capitalism. He seemed to know when enough was enough. He wanted to make money and enough of it to live well, but not so much that he harmed the environment or exploited others. He was philanthropic enough to give away resources that benefited the general populace. There was usually something in it for him, but financial profit wasn't his only motivation.

If he had an Achilles heel, it was that he didn't invest enough of his time and energy in his family life, hence two failed marriages and flawed relationships with his children, with the exception of Mary. He did not have a well-developed enough social conscience to resist the exclusionary clauses in the deeds for Pebble Beach, but he was civic and community-minded enough to leave behind a legacy of numerous good works locally that benefitted all, not just the rich and famous, especially in the environmental arena.

His standards set a tone for the Monterey Peninsula. While some resort communities have been spoiled over the years and lost the flavor that made them attractive in the first place, (Palm Springs comes to mind) for the most part, that hasn't happened here. His imprimatur set in motion a tradition of valuing and preserving the natural beauty of the area coupled with caution about development that exists to this day.

END

Family Charts

The Morse Family Tree

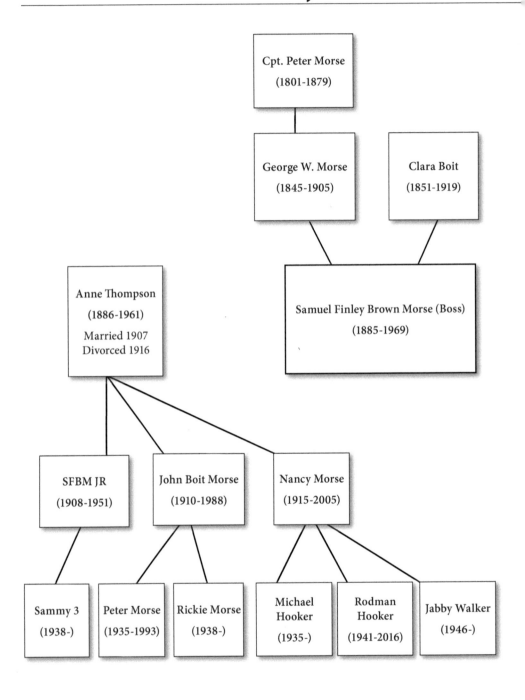

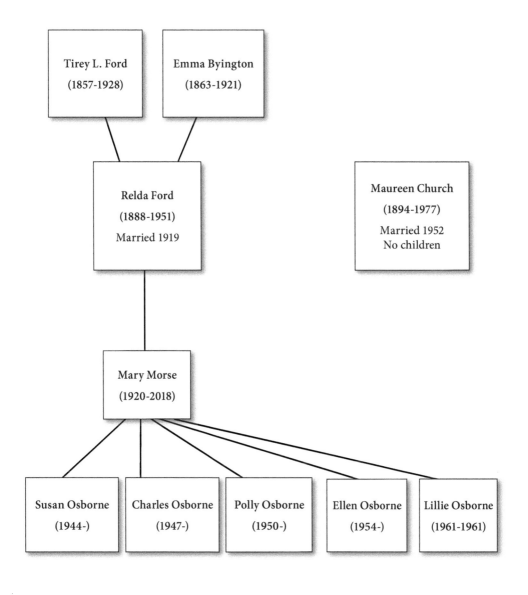

Relationshhip of Samuel Finley Breese Morse
to Samuel Finley Brown Morse

Anthony Morse (1606–1686)
Arrived Newbury Mass in 1634
from Marlborough England

Brothers:	Benjamin (1640–?)	Anthony Jr.(?–1677)
1st cousins:	Benjamin Jr. (1668–1743)	Peter (1674–1721)
2nd cousins:	Hon. Abel (1692–?)	John (1699–1764)
3rd cousins:	Stephen (1723–1807)	Jedediah(1726–1819)
4th cousins:	Peter (1774–1863)	Jedediah (1761–1826)
5th cousins:	Capt. Peter (1801–1879)	**S. F. B. Morse (1791–1872)**
Once removed:	George Washington (1845–1905)	
Twice removed	**Samuel Finley Brown (S.F.B.) Morse (1885–1969)**	

The Crocker Descendants (Partial)

	Charles Crocker (1822–1888)			Edwin Crocker
Brothers				
Children	Charles Frederick	William Henry (1861–1937)	George, Harriet	Aimée Isabella
Grandchildren	Templeton Jenny Harry	Charles Helen William W.		
Great Grandchildren	Frederick Whitman Robert Henderson	Charles III William		
Great-Great Grandchild	Michael Whitman			

Index

People

Places

N

Newtonville, Massachusetts, 1, 5

P

Pacific Grove, 38, 40–41, 42, 52, 64, 96, 106, 120
Pebble Beach, 37, 38, 44–47, 48–53, 86–91, 99–102, 114–119
Pebble Beach Road Races, 118
Phillips Academy, Andover, 1–4

R

Rancho Del Monte, 36
River Ranch, 71–76, 79, 81, 95, 110, 125, 127, 131

S

San Clemente Dam, 52, 64
San Francisco, 1915, 23–25
Stevenson School, 120, 126, 131

T

Temptress, The, 83–85, 91

V

Vileehi, 125
Visalia, California, 16–19

W

White Siren, The, 125
World's Fair, San Francisco, 1915, 23–25

Y

Yale University, 1, 5, 7–11, 13, 16, 20, 84, 103, 126

Photo & Illustration Credits

1: Courtesy Pebble Beach Company Lagorio Archives, © Pebble Beach Company

2: Courtesy Julian P. Graham/Loon Hill Studios

Photograph of the author by Ethan A. Russell